ather Stefano Manelli, O.F.M. Conv., S.T.D.

Jesus Our Eucharistic Love

Eucharistic Life
According to the examples of the Saints

JESUS OUR EUCHARISTIC LOVE
by Father Stefano Manelli, O.F.M. Conv., S.T.D

Father Stefano Manelli has been a priest for about twenty-eight years. For about ten years he was superior of the Friary, "Casa Mariana" (House of Mary) which he founded. This religious community inspired by St. Maximillian Kolbe's idea of the "City of the Immaculate" tries to follow ever more closely the ideals and rule of St. Francis of Assisi .

The printing facilities and radio station of Father Manelli's "Casa Mariana" continue to expand and are used exclusively to make Jesus and Mary better known and loved. Under Father Manelli's leadership Casa Mariana further expanded by starting another House of Mary in the Philippines. Father Manelli in 1982 was elected Provincial of the Conventual Franciscans in Naples.

Father Manelli, who has his Doctorate in Sacred Theology, is well known in Italy. His book, "Jesus Our Eucharistic Love" has gone through at least five editions in Italy and over 100,000 copies have been printed.

Although some of his other works have been published elsewhere in English, this is the first time that this very solid and devout work has been published in North America. Father was pleased to give us permission to publish his work in English as he looks forward to being able to reach even more souls through the mass media to bring them, through Mary to the sweet yoke of Christ. We are happy to publish this book and distribute it.

To all who want to know more and to love more the Divine Love of Our Eucharistic Jesus, we invite you to read this very powerful and edifying book.

CONTENTS

Note: Captions to the pictures have been added

by the English language publishers.

PRINTED IN THE UNITED STATES OF AMERICA

"The devotion to the Eucharist," St. Pius X, the Pope of the Eucharist, said, "is the most noble, because it has God as its object; it is the most profitable for salvation, because It gives us the Author of grace; it is the sweetest, because the Lord is Sweetness Itself."

The devotion to the Eucharist, together with the devotion to the Blessed Mother, is a devotion of paradise, because it is the devotion which the Angels and Saints of Heaven also have. "There is a school in Heaven," the mystic, St. Gemma Galgani, used to say, "and there one has only to learn how to love. The school is in the Cenacle; the Teacher is Jesus; the matter taught is His Flesh and His Blood."

The Eucharist is Love Itself, identical to Jesus. Therefore, it is the Sacrament of Love, the Sacrament that overflows with charity. It truly contains the true, living Jesus -- the God Who "is Love," (John 4:8) and Who loved us "unto the end." (John 13:1)

All expressions of love, even the highest and the most profound, are verified in the Eucharist. Thus, is a Love that is crucified, a Love that unites, a Love that adores, a Love that contemplates, a Love that prays, a Love that delightfully satisfies.

The Eucharistic Jesus is a Love that is crucified in the Most Holy Sacrifice of the Mass, in which He renews the immolation of Himself for us. In sacramental and spiritual communion He is a Love that unites, making Himself one with the person who receives Him. He is a Love that adores in the holy tabernacle, where He is present as a holocaust of adoration to the Father. He is a Love that contemplates in His encounter with souls who love to be at His feet," like Mary of Bethany. (Luke 10:39) He is a Love that prays in "always living to make

5

intercession for us" before the Father. (Hebrew 7:25) He is a Love that delightfully satisfies in th heavenly exhilarations of nuptial union with Hi favored spouses, (virgins of both sexes); whom H draws to Himself in an exclusive Love, as He drev to Himself St. John the Evangelist, the virgin Apostl and the only one who "leaned on His breast" in th Cenacle. (John 21:20)

"To be possessed by Jesus and to possess Him that is the perfect reign of Love," wrote St. Pete Julian Eymard. The Eucharist achieves this "perfec reign of Love" in all, who are pure of heart, approacl the Holy Tabernacle and unite themselves to Jesu in the Host with humility and love. In the Eucharist Jesus sacrifices Himself for us, He gives Himself t us, He remains among us with infinite humility an love.

"For One in such a lofty position to stoop so lov is a marvel that is staggering," exclaimed the Seraphi Father, St. Francis. "What sublime humility an humble sublimeness, that the Lord of the Universe the Divine Son of God, should so stoop as to hid Himself under the appearance of bread for our salva tion! Behold the humble way of God, my brother Therefore, do not hold yourselves to be anything c yourselves, so that you may be entirely acceptabl to One Who gives Himself entirely to you".

And St. Alphonsus Liguori adds with his usua affectionate tenderness, "My Jesus! What a lovabl contrivance this holy Sacrament was -- that Yo would hide under the appearance of bread to mak Yourself loved and to be available for a visit by anv one who desires You!"

May some remembrance of the priest, who ever day gives us Jesus, and of the Blessed Virgin Mary Mother of Jesus our God and all priests, be alway in our affections toward the Most Holy Sacramen for the Eucharist, Our Lady, and the priest are inseparable, just as Jesus, Mary and St. John the Evangelist were inseparable on Calvary.

Let us learn all this in the school of the Saints. They lived in a way that was ardent and sublime, as true seraphims of Love for the Eucharist. These are the ones, as Vatican II declares (Lumen Gentium, n.50), who are the "most safe path" to the Eucharistic God of Love.

Eucharistic Jesus is Emmanuel, that is, "God with us." (Matt. 1:23)

Chapter I
O DIVINE EUCHARIST!

- Eucharistic Jesus is God among us.
- How to know, love and live the Eucharist.

ucharistic Jesus is God Among Us

When St. John Mary Vianney arrived at the obscure little village of Ars, someone said to him with bitterness, "Here there is nothing to do." "Therefore, there is everything to do," replied the Saint.

And he began immediately to act. What did he do? He arose at 2:00 A.M. in the morning and went to pray near the altar in the dark church. He recited the Divine Office, he made his meditation and he prepared himself for Holy Mass. After the Holy Sacrifice, he made his thanksgiving; then he remained at prayer until Noon. He would be always kneeling on the floor without any support, with a rosary in his hand and his eyes fixed on the Tabernacle.

Things continued this way for a short time.

But then ... he had to start changing his timetable; and things reached a point requiring radical changes in his program. The Eucharistic Jesus and the Blessed Virgin Mary, little by little, drew souls to that poor parish, until the Church did not seem big enough to contain the crowds, and the confessional of the holy Curate became swamped with endless lines of penitents. The holy Curate was obliged to hear confessions for ten, fifteen and eighteen hours a day! How did such a transformation ever come about? There had been a poor Church, an altar long unused, an abandoned tabernacle, an ancient confessional and a priest of little talent with no means to do anything. How could these things achieve such a remarkable change in that obscure village?

We can ask the same question today regarding San Giovanni Rotundo, a town in Gargano, Italy. Until a few decades ago it was an obscure, unknown place amid the rough crags of a promontory. Today, San Giovanni Rotundo is a center of spiritual and cultural life and its reputation is international. Here, too, there had been an unpromising, sickly friar, an ancient, dilapidated little Friary, a small neglected Church, with altar and tabernacle left ever alone to this poor friar, who wore out his beads and his hands in the untiring recitation of the Holy Rosary.

How did the change come about? What caused the wonderful transformation that came to Ars and to San Giovanni Rotundo, so that hundreds of thousands, and perhaps millions, of persons have come there from every part of the earth?

Only God could work such transformations using according to His ways, "the things that are not to bring to naught the things that are." (1 Cor. 1:28) It is all due to Him, to the divine and infinite power of the Eucharist, to the almighty force of attraction which radiates from every tabernacle, and which radiated from the tabernacles of Ars and San Giovanni Rotundo, reaching souls through the ministry of those two priests, true "Ministers of the Tabernacles" and "dispensers of the mysteries of God." (1 Cor. 4:1)

Let us ask the question: What is the Eucharist? It is *God among us.* It is the Lord Jesus present in the tabernacles of our churches with His Body, Blood, Soul and Divinity. It is Jesus veiled under the appearance of bread, but really and physically present in the consecrated Host, so that He dwells in our midst works within us and for us, and is at our disposal. The Eucharistic Jesus is the true Emmanuel, the "God with us." (Matt. 1:23)

"The faith of the Church," Pope Pius XII teaches us, "is this: That one and identical is the *Word* of God and the Son of Mary Who suffered on the Cross, Who is present in the Eucharist, and Who rules in Heaven."

The Eucharistic Jesus is here with us as a brother as a friend, as spouse of our souls. He wishes to enter

10

within us to be our food for eternal life, our love, our support. He wants to make us part of His mystical Body in which He would redeem us and save us, and then take us into the kingdom of Heaven to settle us in an everlasting bliss of love.

With the Eucharist, God has truly given us everything. St. Augustine exclaimed: "Although God is all-powerful, He is unable to give more; though supremely wise, He knows not how to give more; though vastly rich, He has not more to give."

To the Eucharist, then, we should go. To Jesus we should turn -- to Jesus, Who wishes to make Himself ours in order to make us His by rendering us "godlike." "Jesus, Food of strong souls," St. Gemma Galgani used to say, "strengthen me, purify me, make me godlike." Let us receive the Eucharist with a pure and ardent heart. This is as the Saints have done. It should never be too much trouble for us to grow familiar with this unspeakable mystery. Meditation, study and reflection on the Eucharist should have an important place each day on our time-table. It will be the time of our day richest in blessings.

Knowing, Loving, Living the Eucharist

In order to explore at least some of the immense riches stored up in the Mystery of the Eucharist, let us undertake an exercise which, while one and constant, uses the mind, the heart and the will.

First, it uses the mind. Here one meditates in an attentive, orderly way on the Eucharist. This may be done with books which lead us to personally uncover and deeply ponder this Mystery of Love. A simple booklet which is rich in content is St. Alphonsus M. de Liguori's *"Visits to the Blessed Sacrament and to the Blessed Virgin Mary."* Also, there are the two precious booklets by St. Peter Julian Eymard entitled, *"The Real Presence"* and *"Holy Communion."*

11

We should, above all, turn to the school of St. Peter Julian Eymard, who was unequalled as an Apostle of the Eucharist. His vocation and mission was to lead all Christians to the Eucharist. When he founded the Congregation of Priests of the Blessed Sacrament, he offered his life for the Eucharistic reign of Jesus. At that time he wrote these ardent words: "Here, dear Jesus, is my life. Behold me ready to eat stones and to die abandoned, just so that I may succeed in erecting a throne for Thee and give Thee a family of friends, a nation of adorers."

If we but knew the gift of God Who is Love and Who gives Himself to us as a Gift full of Love! "The Eucharist," said St. Bernard, "is that love which surpasses all loves in Heaven and on earth." And St. Thomas Aquinas wrote: "The Eucharist is the Sacrament of Love: It signifies Love, It produces Love."

One day an Arabian prince, Abd-ed-Kader, while passing through the streets of Marseille with a French official, met a priest who was carrying Holy Viaticum to a dying man. The French official stopped, uncovered his head, and knelt. His friend asked him the reason for this gesture.

"I adore my God, Whom the priest is carrying to a sick person," replied the good official.

"How is it possible," the prince said, "for you to believe that God Who is so great, makes Himself so little and lets Himself go even to the homes of the poor? We Mohammedans have a much higher idea of God."

The official answered, "It is because you have only an idea of the greatness of God; that you do not know His Love."

In confirmation of this, St. Peter Eymard declares, "The Eucharist is the supreme proof of the love of Jesus. After this, there is nothing more but Heaven itself." Yet, how many of us Christians do not know the vast extent of the love contained in the Eucharist.

Second, to explore the riches of the Eucharist, we use the heart. If every Christian must love Jesus Christ ("If any man love not our Lord Jesus Christ, let him be anathema." 1 Cor. 16:22) Love for the Eucharist must spring from the heart and be ever alive in us all. Now even love needs exercise. The heart needs to be exercised to love the true God, to long for "The Author of Life." (Acts 3:15)

Holy Communion represents the loftiest point of this exercise of love, Whose consuming flames unite the heart of a creature and Jesus. St. Gemma Galgani could exclaim in this regard, "I can no longer avoid the thought that in the wonderful scope of His Love, Jesus makes Himself perceptible and shows Himself to His lowliest creature in all the splendors of His Heart." And what may we say about the "exercises" of the heart of St. Gemma, who desired to be a "tent of love" in which she would keep Jesus always with her? She longed to have a "little place in the ciborium" to be able to stay always with Jesus. She asked that she could become "a flaming ball afire with love" for Jesus.

When St. Therese of the Child Jesus had become quite ill, she dragged herself with great effort to Church to receive Jesus. One morning, after Holy Communion, she was in her cell, exhausted. One of the Sisters remarked that she should not exert herself so much. The Saint replied, "Oh, what are these sufferings to me in comparison with one Holy Communion?" Her sweet complaint was that she could not receive Holy Communion every day. (It was not permitted in her times.) She ardently pleaded with Jesus: "Remain within me, as You do in the Tabernacle. Do not ever withdraw Your presence from Your little Host."

When St. Margaret Mary Alacoque left the world and consecrated herself to God in the cloister, she made a private vow and wrote it in her blood, "All for the Eucharist; nothing for me." It is useless to attempt to describe the Saint's burning love for the Eucharist. When she was not able to receive Holy Communion, she broke out in ardent expressions of love like these: "I have such a desire for Holy Communion that if I had to walk barefoot along a path of fire to obtain It, I would do so with unspeakable joy."

St. Catherine of Sienna said often to her confessor: "Father, I am hungry; for the love of God give this soul her food, her Lord in the Eucharist." She also confided: "When I am not able to receive my Lord, I go into the Church, and there I look at Him . . . I look at Him again . . . and this satisfies me."

This we call "exercise of the heart."

Third, to find the riches of the Eucharist, one should exercise the will. One must do this by bringing the divine lessons of the Eucharist into his life. What good would it be to discover the infinite worth of the Eucharist as we ponder It and seek to love It at Communion time, if we do not then proceed to live It?

The Eucharist teaches a love that goes beyond telling. It teaches total self-sacrifice, and an unequalled lesson in humility and self-effacement. It teaches patience and unrestricted dedication. But what do we draw from all this? We surely ought to achieve something! Can we continue to be indifferent and do nothing when Jesus has loved us and still loves us with this great generosity "even to the end?" (John 13:1)

If we feel frail, we need to turn to Him, to speak to Him and not tarry about asking His help and support, for He is the very One Who said, "Without Me you can do nothing." (John 15:5) First of all let us go be fore Him: "Come to Me . . . and I will refresh you." (Matt.11:28) Let us often visit Him, entering a Church every time we can and pausing a little while before the tabernacle, and put both our heart close to Him and our body before His! The Saints were constantly eager to make visits to Jesus in the Blessed Sacrament, to make Holy Hours of adoration, spiritual communions, ejaculatory prayers and earnest acts of love that come from the heart. How much profit they gained from this and how much good they passed on!

One day in Turin a friend, who was his companion from the University, asked Peter George Frassati, "Let us go and take an appetizer." Peter George **took advantage of the occasion** and replied, indicating to his friend the nearby Church of St. Dominic, "But, of course, let us go and take it in that cafe." Entering the Church, they prayed for a little while near the tabernacle; then they neared the offering box, Peter George said, **"Here is the appetizer."** And from the pockets of the two youths came alms for the poor!

Thinking of the Eucharist during his sermon, St. John Chrysostom asked one time, "How can we make of our bodies a host?" And he himself replied, "Let your eyes look at nothing evil, and you have offered a sacrifice; let not your tongue offer unbecoming words and you have made an offering; let not your hand commit a sin and you have offered a holocaust."

Just recall the eyes of St. Colette, which were always lowered and recollected in sweet modesty. Why? She once gave the answer: "My eyes, I have filled with Jesus upon Whom I have fixed them at the Elevation of the Host at Holy Mass and I do not wish to replace Him with any other image."

Let us think of the reserve and edification of the Saints in speaking, using with exactness the tongue which had been consecrated by contact with the Body of Christ Jesus.

Recall the good works which souls, filled with love by the Eucharist, have accomplished because Jesus communicated to them His own sentiments of love to all the brothers, especially the most needful.

Can we not also exercise thus our will? Let us learn from the Saints and begin to continue their good works.

Padre Pio, the stigmatist priest of Pietrelcina, (above) gave us the example of adoring the Eucharistic Jesus before receiving Him in Holy Communion.

Jesus "has loved me and has sacrificed Himself for me." (Gal. 2:20)

Chapter 2
JESUS FOR ME

- Holy Mass is the Sacrifice of the Cross
- Daily Holy Mass
- Active and fruitful participation
- Holy Mass and the souls in Purgatory

Pope John Paul II reminds us in his homily at Fatima on May 13 1982, that Jesus on the Cross gave Mary to each one of us as our Mother. On the Cross also Jesus sacrificed Himself for our salvation Today Jesus continues to offer Himself to the Eternal Father for our salvation in the Holy Sacrifice of the Mass which is the same sacrifice as the sacrifice of Jesus on the Cross.

Holy Mass is the Sacrifice of the Cross

Only in Heaven will we understand what a divine marvel the Holy Mass is. No matter how much we force ourselves and no matter how holy and inspired we are, we cannot but stammer on this divine work which transcends men and Angels.

One day Padre Pio of Pietrelcina had been asked, "Father, please explain the Holy Mass to us." "My children," replied Padre Pio, "how can I explain it to you? The Mass is infinite like Jesus . . . ask an Angel what a Mass is and he will reply to you in truth, 'I understand what it is and why it is offered, but I do not, however, understand how much value it has.' One Angel, a thousand Angels, all of Heaven, know this and think like this."

St. Alphonsus of Liguori came to affirm, "God Himself cannot bring about an action more holy and greater than the celebration of one Holy Mass." Why? Because the Holy Mass is, one could say, the synthesis, because the Holy Mass can be said to sum up the Incarnation and Redemption and contains the Birth, Passion and the Death of Jesus, mysteries which God accomplished for our sakes. The second Vatican Council teaches, "At the Last Supper, the night in which He was betrayed, Jesus initiated the Eucharistic Sacrifice of His Body and Blood, in order to continue the Sacrifice of the Cross throughout the centuries until His return." (Sacrosantum Concilium, The Constitution on the Liturgy, n.47) St. Thomas Aquinas, in an enlightening passage, wrote, "The celebration of the Holy Mass is as valuable as the death of Jesus on the Cross."

For this reason, St. Francis of Assisi said, "Man should tremble, the world should vibrate, all Heaven should be deeply moved when the Son of God appears on the altar in the hands of the priest."

Indeed, inasmuch as it renews the Sacrifice of Jesus' passion and death, the Holy Mass, even taken alone, is great enough to restrain divine justice. St. Teresa of Jesus said to her daughters, "Without the Holy Mass what would become of us? All here below would perish, because that alone can hold back God's arm." Without it the Church certainly would not last and the world would become hopelessly lost. "It would be easier for the world to survive without the sun than to do so without the Holy Mass," said Padre Pio of Pietrelcina. He was following St. Leonard of Port Maurice who had said, "I believe that if there were no Mass, the world would by now have sunk into the abyss under the weight of its wickedness. The Mass is the powerful support which sustains it."

Wonderful are the saving effects which every Sacrifice of the Mass produces in the souls of those who participate. It obtains sorrow and pardon for sins; it lessens the temporal punishment due to sins; it weakens the influence of Satan and the untamed impulses of our flesh; it strengthens the bonds of our union in the Body of Christ; it protects us from danger and disaster; it shortens the punishment of Purgatory; it obtains for us a higher degree of glory in Heaven. "No human tongue," said St. Laurence Justinian , "can enumerate the favors that trace back to the Sacrifice of the Mass. The sinner is reconciled with God; the just man becomes more upright; sins are wiped away; vices eliminated; virtue and merit gain growth and the devil's schemes are frustrated."

And so St. Leonard of Port Maurice did not tire of exhorting the crowds which listened to him, "O you deluded people, what are you doing? Why do you not hasten to the churches to hear as many Masses as you can? Why do you not imitate the Angel who, when a Holy Mass is celebrated, come down in quadrons from Paradise and take their stations about our altars in adoration to intercede for us?"

If it is true that we all have need of graces for this life and for the next, nothing can win them from God like the Holy Mass. St. Philip Neri used to say, "With prayer we ask graces from God; in the Holy Mass we constrain God to give them to us." The prayer offered during Holy Mass engages our whole priesthood, both the ministerial priesthood even apart from that of the individual priest at the altar and the common priesthood of all the faithful. In Holy Mass our prayer is united with Jesus' prayer of agony as He sacrifices Himself for us. In a special way during the Canon, which is the heart of the Mass, the prayer of all of us becomes also the prayer of Jesus, present amongst us. The two Mementoes of the Roman Canon during which the living and the dead are remembered, are precious moments for us to present our petitions. Also, in those supreme moments when Jesus in the priest's hands undergoes His Passion and Death, we can beg for our own needs and we can recommend both living and deceased persons who are dear to us. Let us take care to profit by this. The Saints held this to be very important, and when they recommended themselves to the prayers of priests, they asked them to remember them above all during the Canon.

It will particularly be at the hour of our death that the Masses we have devoutly heard will bring us our greatest consolation and hope, and one Mass heard during life will be more profitable than many Masses heard by others in our behalf after our death.

Our Lord told St. Gertrude, "You may be sure that regarding one who devoutly assists at Holy Mass, I will send him as many of my Saints to comfort him and protect him during the last moments of his life as there will have been Masses which he has heard well."

How consoling! The Holy Curé of Ars had reason to say, "If we knew the value of the holy Sacrifice of the Mass, how much greater effort we would put forth in order to assist at it!" And St. Peter Julian Eymard exhorted, "Know, O Christian, that the Mass is the holiest act of Religion. You cannot do anything to glorify God more nor profit your soul more than devoutly assisting at It, and assisting as often as possible."

For this reason we must consider ourselves fortunate every time we have an opportunity to attend a Holy Mass; and in order not to lose the opportunity, we should never withhold ourselves because of some sacrifice, especially on Sundays and holy days.

Let us remember St. Maria Goretti, who, to go to Sunday Mass traveled on foot, a journey of 15 miles going and returning home. We should think of Santina Campana, who went to Mass while she had a high fever. Think of Saint Maximilian M. Kolbe, who offered Holy Mass when his health was in such pitiful condition that one of his brothers in religion had to support him at the altar so that he would not fall. And how many times Padre Pio of Pietrelcina celebrated Holy Mass while he was bleeding and had a fever!

In our own daily lives, we ought to rank the Holy Mass ahead of any other good; for, as St. Bernard says, "One merits more by devoutly assisting at a Holy Mass than by distributing all of his goods to the poor and traveling all over the world on pilgrimage." And it cannot be otherwise, because nothing in the world can have the infinite value of one Holy Mass.

We ought to prefer Holy Mass all the more to mere amusements that waste our time and bring no profit to our soul. St. Louis IX, King of France, attended several Masses every day. A minister of the government complained, remarking that he could devote hat time to the affairs of the kingdom. The saintly king remarked, "If I spent twice the time in amusements, like hunting, no one would have any objection."

Let us be generous and willingly make sacrifices so as not to lose so great a good. St. Augustine said to his Christians, "All the steps that one takes as he travels to hear Holy Mass are counted by an angel; and then one will be given a high reward by God in this life and in eternity." The Curé of Ars adds, "How happy is that guardian angel who accompanies a soul to Holy Mass!"

Daily Holy Mass

Once one realizes that Holy Mass has infinite worth, one is not surprised at the Saints' eagerness and care to attend it every day, and even more often insofar as possible.

St. Augustine has left us this praise of his mother, St. Monica, "She did not let a day pass without being present at the divine Sacrifice before Your altar, O Lord."

St. Francis of Assisi usually attended two Masses each day; and when he was sick he asked a friar who was a priest to celebrate Holy Mass for him in his cell so that he would not be without Holy Mass.

Every morning after celebrating Holy Mass, St. Thomas Aquinas served another Mass in thanksgiving.

The shepherd boy, St. Paschal Baylon, could not go to church to attend all the Masses he would have liked because he had to take the sheep to the pasture. So, every time he heard the church bells give the signal for Mass, he knelt on the grass among the sheep before a wooden cross that he had made, and in this way he would, from afar, follow the priest as he offered the divine Sacrifice. What a lovable Saint, a true seraphim of love towards the Eucharist. On his death bed he heard the bell for Mass and had the strength to whisper to his brethren, "I am happy

23

to unite to the Sacrifice of Jesus the sacrifice of my poor life." And he died at the Consecration of Holy Mass.

St. Margaret, Queen of Scotland and mother of eight children, went to Mass every day and brought her children with her, and with motherly care she taught them to treasure the little missal which she chose to adorn with precious stones.

Let us manage our affairs so well that we will not lack time for Holy Mass. Let us not say that we are too busy with chores, for which Jesus could remind us, "Martha, Martha, thou art troubled about many things, but one thing alone is necessary." (Luke 10:41-42).

When one really wants to, one finds time to go to Mass without failing in one's duties. St. Joseph Cottolengo recommended daily Mass for everybody -- for teachers, nurses, laborers, doctors, parents -- and to those who objected that they did not have time to go he replied firmly, "Bad management! Bad economy of time!" He spoke the truth. If we but appreciated the infinite value of the Holy Mass, we would be very desirous of assisting and would try in every way to find the necessary time.

When St. Charles of Sezze was going about Rome seeking alms for his community, he would take time out to make visits to a church to attend additional Masses. It was at the moment of the elevation of the Host during one of these Masses that he received the dart of love into his heart.

Every morning St. Francis of Paula went to church and he remained therein to attend all the daily Masses which were celebrated. St. John Berchmans, St. Alphonsus Rodriguez and St. Gerard Majella used to serve at as many Masses as they could. (They did this with such devotion and edification that they attracted many of the faithful into church.)

Venerable Francis of the Child Jesus, a Carmelite, served at ten Masses every day. If it happened that he had a few less to serve, he would say, "Today I have not had my full breakfast." And what can we say of Padre Pio of Pietrelcina? Padre Pio heard many Masses every day, and participated at them by reciting many Rosaries! The Holy Curé of Ars was not mistaken when he said, "The Mass is the devotion of the Saints."

The same must be said of the love that holy priests have had for celebrating Mass. It was for them a terrible suffering to be unable to celebrate Mass. "When you hear that I cannot celebrate Mass any more, count me as dead," St. Francis Xavier Bianchi said to a brother religious.

St. John of the Cross made it clear that the greatest suffering he had during his ordeal of imprisonment was that of not being able to celebrate Mass nor receive Holy Communion for nine continuous months.

Obstacles and difficulties did not count for the Saints when they were arranging their affairs with a view to not losing so excellent a good. For example, one day in the streets of Naples, St. Alphonsus Liguori suffered violent pains in the abdomen. The religious who accompanied him urged him to stop and take a sedative. But the Saint had not yet celebrated Mass and his prompt response was, "My dear brother, I would walk ten miles in this condition in order not to miss saying Holy Mass." And his sufferings would not move him to break the Eucharistic fast which at that time was obligatory from midnight. He waited until the pain subsided a little and then continued his walk to church.

The Capuchin, St. Laurence of Brindisi, found himself in a town of heretics. Since this town had no Catholic Church, he journeyed forty miles on foot to reach a chapel cared for by Catholics in which he was able to celebrate Holy Mass.

St. Francis de Sales one time was staying in a Protestant town, and to celebrate Holy Mass he had to go every morning before dawn to a Catholic parish church which was on the other side of a broad stream. During the autumn rains the stream rose more than usual and washed away the little bridge on which the Saint had been crossing. But St. Francis was not disheartened. He threw a large beam in the place where the bridge had been and continued to cross over. In winter, however, because of the ice and snow, there was serious danger of his slipping and falling into the water. The Saint then devised a procedure whereby he put himself astride the beam and then manoeuvered across on all fours, so that he might not miss his celebration of Holy Mass.

We will never succeed in sufficiently pondering that mystery beyond description, the Holy Mass, which reproduces on our altars the Sacrifice of Calvary. Nor can we ever have too much devotion for this supreme marvel of Divine Love.

"Holy Mass," wrote St. Bonaventure, "is an achievement of God wherein He places before our view all the love He has borne us; in a sense it is the synthesis, the sum of all benefits bestowed upon us."

Active and Fruitful Participation

The infinite greatness of the Holy Mass should enable us to understand the need of attentively and devoutly taking part in the Sacrifice of Jesus. Adoration, love and sorrow ought to have undisputed predominance among our sentiments.

In a very moving reflection, quoted forcefully by Vatican II, Pope Pius XII portrayed the disposition with which one should take part in the Holy Mass; that is, it should be with "the dispositions that the

Divine Redeemer had when He sacrificed Himself--the same humble spirit of submission--that is, of adoration, love, praise and thanksgiving to the great majesty of God..., so that we reproduce in ourselves the condition of victimhood, the self-denial that follows the Gospel's teaching, whereby of our own accord we make the willing sacrifice of penance, sorrow and expiation for our sins."

True, active participation at Holy Mass is what makes us into slain victims like Jesus and succeeds in "reproducing in us the pain-marked features, the suffering likeness of Jesus" (Pius XII), allowing us "the fellowship of His sufferings" as we are "made conformable to His death" (Philippians 3:10). All the rest is simply liturgical ceremony, simply clothing. St. Gregory the Great taught: "The Sacrifice of the altar will be on our behalf truly acceptable as our offering to God when we present ourselves as victims." As a reflection of this doctrine, in early Christian communities the faithful used to advance in penitential garb, chanting the litany of the Saints, in a procession to the altar for the celebration of Holy Mass, with the Pope presiding. If we would go to Mass in this spirit, we should want to make our own the sentiment St. Thomas the Apostle expressed when he said, "Let us also go, that we may die with Him" (John 11:16).

When St. Margaret Mary Alacoque attended Holy Mass, as she gazed at the altar, she would never fail to take a glance at the Crucifix and the lighted candles. Why? It was to impress into her mind and heart two things: the **Crucifix** reminded her of what Jesus had done for her; the **lighted candles** recalled what she must do for Jesus; that is, sacrifice herself and consume herself for Him and for souls.

The best example of participation at the Holy Sacrifice is given us at the foot of the Cross by the most Blessed Virgin Mary, St. John the Evangelist and St. Mary Magdalen with the pious women (John 19:25). To assist at Mass is very much like being at Calvary.

St. Andrew Avellino used to be moved to tears as he said, "One cannot separate the most Holy Eucharist from the Passion of Jesus."

One day a spiritual son asked Padre Pio of Pietrelcina, "Father, how should we take part at Holy Mass?"

Padre Pio replied, "As Our Lady, St. John and the pious women did on Calvary, loving Him and showing Him pity."

In a missal of one of his spiritual children Padre Pio wrote: "In assisting at Holy Mass, concentrate intently on the tremendous mystery which is taking place before your eyes, and that is the Redemption and reconciliation of your soul with God." At another time he was asked, "Father, why is it that you cry so much during Mass?" "My daughter," replied Padre Pio, "what are those few tears compared to what takes place at the altar? There should be torrents of tears!" And still another time it was said to him, "Father, how much you must suffer by standing on the bleeding wounds of your feet for the entire time of Mass!" Padre Pio replied, "During Mass I am not standing, I am hanging." What a reply! The few words, "I am hanging," very strongly express what it is to be "crucified with Christ" of which St. Paul speaks (Gal. 2:19), and which distinguishes the true and full participation at Mass from the vain, academic, even to the point of only noisy external verbal participation. St. Bernadette Soubirous spoke well when she said to a new priest, "Remember that the priest at the altar is always Jesus Christ on the cross." St. Peter of Alcantara vested for Holy Mass as though he were about to go up on Calvary, because all the priestly vestments have a referral to the Passion and Death of Jesus; the alb recalls the white tunic which Herod made Jesus wear in order to mock Him as crazy; the cord recalls the scourging of Jesus; the stole recalls the rope which tied Jesus; the tonsure recalls the crowning with thorns; the chasuble, signed with the sign of the cross, recalls the cross on the shoulders of Jesus.

Those who have assisted at the Mass of Padre Pio recall those burning tears of his; they recall his forceful request that those present follow Holy Mass on their knees; they recall the impressive silence in which the sacred rite unfolded; they recall the distressing suffering which showed itself spontaneously on Padre Pio's face when he pronounced with great effort the words of Consecration; they remember the fervor of the silent prayer of the faithful which filled the church while Padre Pio, silently, prayed several Rosaries for over one hour.

But the suffering participation of Padre Pio at Holy Mass is the same of all the Saints. The tears of Padre Pio were like those of St. Francis of Assisi (which at times became bloody), like those of St. Vincent Ferrer, of St. Ignatius, of St. Philip Neri, of St. Laurence of Brindisi (who at times soaked seven handkerchiefs with his tears), of St. Veronice Juliani, of St. Joseph of Cupertino, of St. Alphonsus, of St. Gemma Galgani .... But, after all, how is it possible to remain indifferent before the Crucifixion and Death of Jesus? We shall certainly not be like the Apostles who slept in Gethsemane and much less shall we be like the soldiers who, at the foot of the Cross, thought only of the game of dice, heedless of the atrocious spasms of Jesus dying! (And yet, this is the distressing impression that we get when seeing a so-called "rock" Mass, celebrated to the rhythm of guitars playing profane and cheap tunes with women in indecent clothes and youths in the most strange fashions... "Lord, pardon them!")

Let us watch the Blessed Virgin and the Saints. Let us imitate them. Only by following them are we on the right road, the road which "has pleased God" (1 Cor. 1:21).

Holy Mass and the Souls in Purgatory

Once we have left this world, there is nothing we will desire more than the celebration of Holy Mass for our souls. The Holy Sacrifice of the Altar is the most powerful intercessory prayer, for it surpasses every prayer, every penance and every good work. Nor will it be difficult for us to understand that if we

"The best example of participation at the Holy Sacrifice is given us at the foot of the Cross by the Most Blessed Virgin Mary, St. John the Evangelist and St. Mary Magdalen ... To assist at Mass is very much like being at Calvary." - Father Manelli

recall that the Sacrifice of the Mass is the same Sacrifice of Jesus which He offered on the Cross and which He now offers on the altar with its infinite expiatory value. Jesus immolated, is the true Victim of "Propitiation for our sins" (1 John 2:2) and His Divine Blood is effused "unto remission of sins" (Matt. 26:28). Absolutely nothing can be equalled to Holy Mass, and the salutary fruits of the Sacrifice can be extended to an unlimited number of souls.

One time, during the celebration of Holy Mass in the Church of St. Paul at the Three Fountains in Rome, St. Bernard saw an unending stairway which went up to Heaven. Very many angels went up and down on it, carrying from Purgatory to Paradise the souls freed by the Sacrifice of Jesus, renewed by priests on the altars all over the world.

Thus, at the death of one of our relatives, let us take much more care about having celebrated, and assisting at, Holy Masses for him, rather than about the flowers, the dark clothes and the funeral procession ...

There are recounted many apparitions of souls being purified in Purgatory who came to ask Padre Pio to offer Holy Mass for their intentions so that they would be able to leave Purgatory. One day he celebrated Holy Mass for the father of one of his fellow Franciscan brothers. At the end of the Holy Sacrifice, Padre Pio said to his brother, "This morning the soul of your father has entered into Heaven." The brother was very happy to hear that, yet he said to Padre Pio, "But, Father, my good father died thirty-two years ago." "My son," Padre Pio replied, 'before God everything is paid for." And it is Holy Mass which obtains for us a price of infinite value: The Body and the Blood of Jesus, the "Immaculate Lamb" (Apoc. 5:12)

During a sermon one day, the Holy Curé of Ars gave the example of a priest who, celebrating Mass for his deceased friend, after the Consecration prayed as follows, "Holy and Eternal Father, let us make an exchange. You possess the soul of my friend in Purgatory; I have the Body of Your Son in my hands. You liberate for me my friend, and I offer to You, Your Son, with all the merits of His Passion and Death."

Let us remember: All prayers and good works offered for a soul are good and commendable, but when we can, let us above all have celebrated Holy Masses (especially the Thirty Gregorian Masses), for the souls of the deceased who are dear to us.

In the life of Blessed Henry Suso we read that as a young man he had made this agreement with a brother of his religious order, "Whichever one of us outlives the other, let him hasten the glory of the one who has passed into eternity with the celebration of one Holy Mass every week." The companion of Blessed Henry died first in a mission territory. Blessed Henry remembered his promise for a little while, then, because he had been obliged to celebrate Masses for others, he substituted the weekly Mass which he had promised his friend with prayers and penances. But his friend appeared to him and scolded him, "Your prayers and your penances are not sufficient for me, I need the Blood of Jesus," "because it is with the Blood of Jesus that we pay the debts of our sins" (Col. 1:14).

Also, the great St. Jerome has written that "for every Mass devoutly celebrated many souls leave Purgatory and they fly to Heaven." The same must be said for Holy Masses devoutly heard. St. Mary Magdalen of Pazzi, the well-known Carmelite mystic, was in the habit of mentally offering the Blood of Jesus for the purpose of freeing the souls in Purga-

ory, and in an ecstasy Jesus showed her that truly
many souls in Purgatory were liberated by the
offering of the Precious Blood. Nor could it be otherwise because, as St. Thomas Aquinas teaches, that
just one drop of the Blood of Jesus with Its infinite
value, can save the whole universe from every
offence.

Let us, therefore, pray for the souls in Purgatory,
and free them from their pains by having celebrated
and hearing many Holy Masses. "All good works
taken together," said the holy Curé of Ars, "cannot
have the value of one Holy Mass, because they are
the works of men, whereas the Holy Mass is the work
of God."

their ordination, priests are told by their Bishop to imitate Our Lord. This
should be especially notable when the priest celebrates Holy Mass.

He who eats My Flesh and drinks My Blood abides
me and I in him" (John 6:57).

Chapter 3
JESUS IN ME

FILIUS MARIAE VIRGINIS

In Holy Communion Jesus gives Himself to me and becomes mine, all mine, in His Body, Blood, Soul and Divinity. Thus, one day, St. Gemma Galgani said candidly to Jesus, "I am Your master."

With Communion, Jesus enters my heart and remains corporally present in me as long as the species (he appearance) of bread lasts; that is, for about 5 minutes. During this time, the Holy Fathers teach that the angels surround me to continue to adore Jesus and love Him without interruption. "When Jesus is corporally present within us, the angels surround us as a guard of love," wrote St. Bernard.

Perhaps we think too little about the sublimity of every Holy Communion, and yet, St. Pius X said that "if the Angels could envy, they would envy us for Holy Communion." And St. Madeleine Sophie Barat defined Holy Communion as "Paradise on earth."

All the saints have understood by experience the divine marvel of the meeting and the union with Jesus in the Eucharist. They have understood that a devout Holy Communion means to be possessed by Him and to possess Him. "He who eats My Flesh and drinks My Blood abides in Me and I in him" (John 6:57). One time St. Gemma Galgani wrote, "It is now night, tomorrow morning is approaching and then Jesus will possess me and I will possess Jesus." It is not possible to have a union of love more profound and more total: He in me and I in Him; the one in the other. What more could we want?

"You envy," said St. John Chrysostom, "the opportunity of the woman who touched the vestments of Jesus, of the sinful woman who washed His feet with her tears, of the women of Galilee who had the happiness of following Him in His pilgrimages, of the Apostles and disciples who conversed with Him familiarly, of the people of the time who listened to the words of grace and salvation which came forth from His lips. You call happy those who saw Him ... But, come to the altar and you will see Him, you will touch Him, you will give to Him holy kisses, you will wash Him with your tears, you will carry Him within you like Mary Most Holy."

For this reason the saints have desired and longed for Holy Communion with ardent love; for example St. Francis of Assisi, St. Catherine of Siena, St. Paschal Baylon, St. Veronica, St. Gerard, St. Margaret Mary Alacoque, St. Dominic Savio, St. Gemma Galgani ... it is pointless to continue because one would really need to list all the saints.

For example, it happened one night to St. Catherine of Genoa, that she dreamed that the following day she would not be able to receive Holy Communion. The sorrow that she experienced was so great that she cried unceasingly, and when she woke up the next morning she found that her face was all wet from the tears she shed in her dream.

St. Theresa of the Child Jesus has written a little Eucharistic Poem, "Desires near the Tabernacle, in which, among other beautiful things, she said "I would like to be the chalice, there where I would adore the Divine Blood. I can however in the Holy Sacrifice, gather It in me every morning. My soul is therefore more dear to Jesus, it is more precious than vessels of gold." And what was not the happiness of the angelic Saint when, during an epidemic, daily Communion was conceded to her?

St. Gemma Galgani, one time was put to the test by a confessor who forbade her to receive Holy Communion. "O Father, Father," she wrote to her spiritual director, "today I went to Confession and he confessor has said that I must stop receiving esus. O my Father, my pen does not want to write nore, my hand shakes strongly, I cry." Dear Saint! Truly a seraphim all on fire with love for the Eucharistic Jesus.

Similarly, St. Gerard Majella, for a false and slanderous report from which he did not wish to defend imself, was punished by being deprived of Holy ommunion. The suffering of the Saint was such that ne day he refused to go to serve Holy Mass for a riest who was visiting, "because," he said, "on seeing esus in the Host in the hands of the priest, I would ot be able to resist taking by force the Host from is hands." What longing consumed this wonderful aint! And what a rebuke for us who, perhaps, are ole to receive Holy Communion daily with ease nd we do not do it. It is a sign that we lack the ssential: love. And perhaps we are so in love with arthly pleasures that we can no longer appreciate ne heavenly delights of union with Jesus in the ost. "Child, how can you feel the fragrance of aradise which diffuses Itself from the Tabernacle?" sked St. Philip of a young man in love with the easures of the flesh, of dances and amusements. he joys of the Eucharist and the satisfaction of e senses are "opposed to each other" (Gal. 5:17) nd the "sensual man perceives not these things hich are of the Spirit of God" (1 Cor. 2:14). This wisdom which comes from God.

St. Philip Neri loved the Eucharist so much that, en when he was gravely ill, he received Holy Communion every day, and if Jesus was not brought to m very early in the morning he became very upset d he could not find rest in any way. "I have such a sire to receive Jesus," he exclaimed, "that I cannot ve myself peace while I wait." The same thing took ace in our own time to Padre Pio of Pietrelcina, since only obedience could make him wait until 4 or 5 a.m. to celebrate Mass. Truly, the love of God is a "Devouring Fire (Deut. 4:24).

When Jesus is mine, the whole Church exalts, the church in Heaven, in Purgatory and the church on earth. Who can express the joy of the Angels and Saints at every Holy Communion devoutly received? A new current of love arrives in Paradise and it makes the blessed spirits vibrate every time that a creature unites himself to Jesus to possess Him and be possessed by Him. A Holy Communion is of much greater value than an ecstasy, a rapture or a vision. Holy Communion transports the whole of Paradise into my poor heart!

For the souls in Purgatory then, Holy Communion is the dearest personal gift which they can receive from us. Who can say how much Holy Communions are helpful in their liberation? One day St. Mary Magdalene of Pazzi's dead father appeared to her and he said that one hundred and seven Holy Communions were necessary for him to be able to leave Purgatory. In fact, at the last of the one hundred and seven Holy Communions offered for him, the saint saw her father ascend into Heaven.

St. Bonaventure made himself an apostle of this truth and he spoke of it in vibrant tones, "O Christian souls, do you wish to prove your true love toward your dead? Do you wish to send them the most precious help and golden key to Heaven? Receive Holy Communion often for the repose of their souls."

Finally, let us reflect that in Holy Communion we unite ourselves not only to Jesus but also to all the members of the Mystical Body of Christ, especially to the souls most dear to Jesus and most dear to our heart. It is in Holy Communion that we realize fully the words of Jesus, "I in them ... that they may be perfect in unity" (John 17:23). The Eucharist renders

40

us one, even among ourselves, His members, "all one in Jesus" as St. Paul says (Gal. 3:28). Holy Communion is truly all love of God and neighbour. It is the true "feast of love," as St. Gemma Galgani said. And in this "feast of Love" the soul in love can exult singing with St. John of the Cross, "Mine are the heavens and mine is the earth, mine are men, the Just are mine and sinners are mine. The Angels are mine, and also the Mother of God, all things are mine. God Himself is mine and for me because Christ is mine and all for me."

The Purity of Soul Necessary for Holy Communion

What is there to say about the great purity of soul with which the saints approached to receive the Bread of Angels? We know that they had a great delicacy of conscience which was truly angelic. Aware of their own misery, they tried to present themselves to Jesus "holy and immaculate," (Eph. 1:4) repeating with the Publican, "O God, be merciful to me a sinner" (Luke 18:13), and having recourse with great care to the cleansing of Confession.

When St. Jerome was brought Holy Viaticum at the end of his life, the Saint prostrated himself on the ground in adoration and he was heard to repeat with profound humility the words of St. Elizabeth and those of St. Peter, "How is this, that my Lord should come to me?" "Depart from me, for I am a sinful man, O Lord" (Luke 5:8). And how many times was the angelic and seraphic St. Gemma tempted to not receive Holy Communion, holding herself to be nothing else than a vile "dunghill?"

Padre Pio of Pietrelcina used to repeat with trepidation to his brethren, "God sees blights even in the angels. What must He see in me!" For this reason he was very diligent in making his sacramental Confessions.

"Oh, if we could only understand Who is that God Whom we receive in Holy Communion, then what purity of heart we would bring to Him!" exclaimed St. Mary Magdalen of Pazzi.

For this reason St. Hugh, St. Thomas Aquinas, St. Francis de Sales, St. Ignatius, St. Charles Borromeo, St. Francis Borgia, St. Louis Bertrand, St. Joseph Cupertino, St. Leonard of Port Maurice and many other saints went to Confession **every day** before celebrating Holy Mass.

St. Camillus de Lellis never celebrated Holy Mass without first going to Confession, because he wanted at least "to dust off" his soul. Once, at sundown in a public square in Livorno, before taking leave of a priest of the same religious order, forseeing that he would not have a priest to confess to on the following morning before his Mass, paused, took off his hat, made the sign of the Cross and went to Confession right there in the square to his confrere.

Also, St. Alphonsus, St. Joseph Cafasso, St. John Bosco, St. Pius X, and Padre Pio of Pietrelcina went to Confession very often. And why did St. Pius X wish to lower the age for First Holy Communion to seven years, if not to allow Jesus to enter into the innocent hearts of children, which are so similar to angels. And why was Padre Pio so delighted when they brought him children five years old who were prepared for First Holy Communion?

The saints applied to perfection the directive of the Holy Spirit, "Let everyone first examine himself, and then eat of that Bread and drink of that Chalice; because he who eats and drinks unworthily, eats and drinks unto his own condemnation" (1 Cor. 11:28-29).

To examine themselves, to repent, to accuse themselves in Confession and to ask pardon of God, and in this way even every day profit from the Sacrament of

Confession, was something natural for the saints. How fortunate they were to be capable of so much! The fruits of sanctification were constant and abundant because the purity of soul with which each saint welcomed into himself Jesus, "the Wheat of the elect," (Zach. 9:17) was like the good ground " ... which brings forth fruit in patience" (Luke 8:15).

St. Anthony Mary Claret illustrates this fact very well: "When we go to Holy Communion, all of us receive the same Lord Jesus, but not all receive the same grace nor are the same effects produced in all. This comes from our greater or lesser disposition. To explain this fact, I will take an example from nature. Consider the process of grafting, the more similar the one plant is to the other, the better the graft will succeed. Likewise, the more resemblance there is between the one that goes to Communion and Jesus, so much the better will the fruits of Holy Communion be." The Sacrament of Confession is in fact the excellent means whereby the similarity between the soul and Jesus is restored.

For this reason St. Francis de Sales taught his spiritual children, "Go to Confession with humility and devotion ... if it is possible, every time that you go to Holy Communion, even though you do not feel in your conscience any remorse of mortal sin."

In this regard it is well to recall the teaching of the Church. Holy Communion must be received only while one is in the grace of God. Therefore, when one has committed a mortal sin, even if one has repented of it and has a great desire to receive Holy Communion, it is **necessary** and **indispensible** to confess oneself first before receiving Holy Communion, otherwise one commits a most grave sin of **sacrilege,** for which Jesus said to St. Bridget, **"there does not exist on earth a punishment which is great enough to punish it sufficiently!"**

St. Ambrose said that persons who commit this sacrilege "come into church with a few sins, and leave it burdened with many." St. Cyril wrote something yet stronger: "They who make a sacrilegious Communion receive Satan and Jesus Christ into their hearts - Satan, that they may let him rule, and Jesus Christ, that they may offer Him in sacrifice as a Victim to Satan." Thus the Catechism of the Council of Trent (De Euch., v.i) declares: "As of all the sacred mysteries ... none can compare with the ... Eucharist, so likewise for no crime is there heavier punishment to be feared from God than for the unholy or irreligious use by the faithful of that which ... contains the very Author and Source of holiness."

On the other hand, Confession made before Holy Communion to render a soul already in the state of Sanctifying Grace more pure and more beautiful, is something precious even though not required. It is precious because it clothes the soul with a more beautiful "wedding garment" (cf. Matt. 22:12) with which it may take its place at the table of the angels. For this reason the most conscientious souls have always made frequent use (at least once a week) of the sacramental cleansing of absolution, even for venial sins. If you want great purity of soul in order to receive Jesus, no purity shines brighter than that which one obtains when he makes a good confession, where the cleansing Blood of Jesus renders the repentant soul divinely bright and beautiful. "The soul that receives the Divine Blood becomes beautiful, as being clothed in a more precious garment, and it appears so beautifully aglow that if you could see it you would be tempted to adore it," declared St. Mary Magdalene di Pazzi.

Holy Communion with Mary

Oh, how much it pleases Jesus to be received by a soul cleansed and clothed with His Divine Blood! And what affectionate delight He takes when such a soul is a chaste virgin! For "the Eucharist came from the Paradise of Virginity" (namely, Mary), said St. Albert the Great; and our Eucharistic Lord does not find such a paradise except in virginity. No one can repeat, quite like a virgin, with the Spouse of the Canticle of Canticles at every Holy Communion: "All mine is my true Love, and I am all His; ... He goes out to pasture among the lilies ... Come back, my heart's Love" (Cant. 2:16 - 17).

One praiseworthy way of preparing for Holy Communion is to invoke the Immaculate Virgin, to count on Her to enable us to receive Jesus with Her humility, Her purity and Her love - praying rather that She Herself may come to receive Him in us. This pious practice is much recommended by the saints, in particular St. Louis Grignon de Montfort, St. Peter Eymard, St. Alphonsus Liguori, and Saint Maximilian Mary Kolbe. "The best preparation for Holy Communion is that which is made with Mary," wrote St. Peter Eymard. A delightful illustration is given by St. Therese of Lisieux, picturing her soul as a little three or four-year old girl whose hair and dress were in disarray, ashamed to present herself at the altar rail to receive Jesus. However she appeals to the Madonna, and "immediately," the Saint writes, "the Virgin Mary occupies Herself with me. She quickly replaces my dirty dress, ties up my hair with a pretty ribbon and adds a simple flower ... This is enough to make me attractive and enables me to take my place without embarrassment at the banquet of the angels."

Let us try this method of preparation. We will not be disappointed. We will be able to say what St. Gemma exclaimed in ecstasy, "How beautiful it is to receive Communion with the Mother of Paradise!"

Thanksgiving After Holy Communion

The time of Thanksgiving after Holy Communion is the most ideal time for an intimate exchange of love with Jesus. Let it be a love of total self-giving thus returning Jesus' love so wholeheartedly that there is no longer two of us but one, so to speak, in soul and body. Let it be a love that vivifies and unites, — He in me and I in Him, so that we may be consumed in the uniqueness and unity of His love.

"You are my loving prey just as I am the object of Your immense charity," said St. Gemma to Jesus with tenderness.

St. John wrote, "Blessed are they that are called to the wedding banquet of the Lamb" (Apoc. 19:9). In

truth, in Eucharistic Communion rightly received, the soul realizes, in a heavenly virginal union, a nuptial love for the Spouse, Jesus, to Whom the soul can say with the most tender enthusiasm of the Bride in the Canticle of Canticles: "Let Him kiss me with the kiss of His mouth" (Cant. 1:1).

Thanksgiving after Holy Communion is a small foretaste, while on earth, of the love which will be experienced in Paradise. In Heaven, in fact, how shall we love Jesus if not by being one with Him eternally? Dear Jesus, sweet Jesus, oh how I ought to thank You for every Holy Communion that You grant me! Did not St. Gemma have good reason to say she would thank You in Paradise for the Eucharist more than for anything else? What a miracle of love to be so completely united with You, O Jesus!

Water, yeast, wax

St. Cyril of Alexandria, Father of the Church, used three illustrations to show the union of love with Jesus in Holy Communion: "He who receives Communion is made holy and Divinized in soul and body in the same way that water, set over a fire, becomes boiling. ...Communion works like yeast that has been mixed into dough so that it leavens the whole mass: ...Just as by melting two candles together you get one piece of wax, so, I think, one who receives the Flesh and Blood of Jesus is fused together with Him by this Communion, and the soul finds that he is in Christ and Christ is in him."

For this reason St. Gemma Galgani used to speak in awed wonder of the Eucharistic union between "Jesus Who is All and Gemma who is nothing." In an ecstasy she exclaimed, "What great sweetness there is, O Jesus, in Communion! I want to live in Your embrace and die in Your embrace." And Blessed Contardo Ferrini wrote, "Ah, Holy Communion! unspeakable heights for a human spirit to reach! What does the world have that equals these pure, heavenly joys, these tastes of eternal glory?"

There is another value Holy Communion has that deserves our reflections, and it is in reference to the Blessed Trinity. One day St. Mary Magdalene di Pazzi was kneeling with arms crossed among the novices after Communion. She raised her eyes heavenward and said, "O Sisters, if only we would comprehend the fact that while the Eucharistic Species remain within us, Jesus is there and working in us inseparably with the Father and the Holy Spirit and therefore the whole Holy Trinity is there---" She could not finish speaking because she became wrapt in ecstasy.

Remain at least fifteen minutes

The Saints chose, when it was possible, to set no time limit for thanksgiving after Communion, which would last at least a half hour. St. Teresa of Jesus told her daughters, "Let us detain ourselves lovingly with Jesus and not waste the hour that follows Communion. It is an excellent time to deal with God and put before Him the matters that concern our soul. ...As we know that good Jesus remains within us until our natural warmth has dissolved the bread-like qualities, we should take great care not to lose such a beautiful opportunity to treat with Him and lay our needs before Him."

St. Francis of Assisi, St. Juliana Falconieri, St. Catharine, St. Paschal, St. Veronica, St. Joseph Cupertino, St. Gemma, and many others, used to almost always go into a loving ecstasy immediately after Holy Communion. As for the duration, only the angels measured the time. Also St. Teresa of Avila nearly always went into ecstasy right after receiving Holy Communion, and sometimes it was necessary to carry her away bodily from the Communion grille

St. John of Avila, St. Ignatius Loyola, and St. Aloysius Gonzaga used to make their thanksgiving on their knees for two hours. St. Mary Magdalene di Pazzi wanted it to continue without interruption. It was necessary to constrain her so that she might take a little nourishment. "The minutes that follow Communion," the Saint said, "are the most precious we have in our lives. They are the minutes best suited on our part for treating with God, and on His part for communicating His love to us."

St. Louis Grignon de Montfort used to remain for Thanksgiving after Holy Mass at least a half hour, and he would not let there be any worry or engagement that could make him omit it. He said, "I would not give up this hour of Thanksgiving even for an hour of Paradise."

Let us also then make the following resolutions: That we will so organize our time and our lives that we will remain in Thanksgiving after Holy Communion for at least fifteen minutes; And further resolve to allow nothing to stop us from taking this time for Thanksgiving. These minutes in which Jesus is physically present to our souls and within our bodies are heavenly minutes that we should by no means waste.

St. Philip and the candles

The Apostle, St. Paul, wrote, "Glorify and bear God in your body" (I Cor. 6:20). There is no time in which these words, taken literally, apply so well, as during the time immediately after receiving Holy Communion. How unfeeling it is, then, for someone to receive Communion and leave the church at once as soon as Mass is over, or as soon as he has received Our Lord! We may remember the example of St. Philip Neri, who had two altar boys with lighted candles go to accompany a man who had left the church right after his Communion. --What a beautiful lesson! For the sake of good manners, if for no other reason, when a person receives a guest he pauses to give his attention to him and takes interest in him. If this guest is Jesus, then we will only have reason to be sorry that His bodily presence within us scarcely lasts fifteen minutes or a little more. In view of this, St. Joseph Cottolengo used to personally oversee the baking of hosts for Mass and Communion. To the sister assigned to this he gave the following instruction: "Make the hosts thick so that I can linger a long time with Jesus. I do not want the Sacred Species to quickly dissolve."

Are we not perhaps acting contrary to the example of the Saints when we regard our period of Thanksgiving as too long and perhaps feel impatient to get it over with? But, oh how we should watch ourselves here! For if it is true that at every Communion Jesus "gives us a hundredfold for the hospitality we show Him," as St. Teresa of Jesus declares, then it is likewise true that we must answer a hundredfold for neglecting this hospitality. A fellow Capuchin of Padre Pio of Pietrelcina told how one day he went to Confession to the holy friar, and, among other things, confessed omitting his Thanksgiving after Holy Mass because, he said, some ministry made him unable. While Padre Pio was lenient in judging the other faults, when he heard him confess this omission, he grew more serious, and, with a stern look, he said firmly "Let us see to it that our being unable is not just being unwilling. I always have to make my Thanksgiving; otherwise I pay dearly."

Let us give the matter serious thought and attention. When it comes to something so very precious a this Thanksgiving, let us take to heart the Holy Spirit's admonition, "Let not your share of desired good pass you by" (Ecclus. 14:14).

Thanksgiving with the Madonna

There is a special beauty in a Thanksgiving made in Mary's company in honour of Her Annunciation. Right after Holy Communion we carry Jesus within our souls and bodies, just as the Blessed Virgin Mary did when She had received the message of the angel. We cannot find a better way to adore and love Jesus at that time than by making our dispositions agree with those of the Mother of God, making our own the same sentiments of adoration and love that She had toward Her Divine Son Jesus enclosed under Her Immaculate Heart. It can be helpful in achieving this, to recite meditatively the Joyful Mysteries of the Rosary. Let us try it. We cannot fail to profit by becoming united this way with the Madonna in order to love Jesus with Her Heavenly Heart.

The Bread of the Strong and Viaticum for Heaven

It ought not to be necessary to say that for everybody, Christ in the Eucharist is the true **Bread to**

make them strong. It is the nourishment to make men heroic, to sustain martyrs, and to bring strength and peace to souls in their last agony.

In the Eucharist, Jesus repeats to us, who suffer and moan in this valley of tears, this affectionate summons, "Come to Me, all you that labor and are burdened, and I will refresh you" (Matt. 11:28). For certainly "The life of man upon earth is a warfare" (Job 7:1). Moreover, Jesus' followers "shall suffer persecution" (cf. II Tim. 3:12; Matt. 5:10); and it is true that they that are Christ's "have crucified their flesh with its passions and concupiscences" (Gal. 5:24), and that we ought to live as dead "with Christ to the elements of the world" (Col. 2:20).

It is also true that with Jesus "I can do all things in Him Who strengthens me" (Phil. 4:13); for Jesus is "all" (cf. John 1:3; Col. 1:17). In Holy Communion He makes Himself "all mine." I can, then, say with the Servant of God. Luisa M. Claret de la Touche, "What need I fear? He Who sustains the world is with in me. The Blood of a God circulates within my veins. Have no fear, O my soul. The Lord of the Universe has taken you up into His Arms and wants you to find rest in Him."

Hence, St. Vincent de Paul was able to ask his missionaries, "When you have received Jesus into your hearts, can any sacrifice be impossible for you?" And St. Vincent Ferrer, during the two years he had to suffer in prison as a victim of persecution, exceedingly abounded with joy in all his tribulations (cf. I Cor. 7:4), because he managed to be able to celebrate Holy Mass every day in spite of his fetters and chains and the darkness of his dungeon. The same fortitude and joy was given to St. Joan of Arc when she was allowed to receive Jesus in the Holy Eucharist before going to her execution at the stake. When Jesus entered her dark prison, the Saint fell on her knees d, wearing her chains, received Jesus, and became sorbed in prayer. As soon as she was bidden to go rth to her death, she rose and made her journey thout interrupting her prayer. She proceeded to the ake and died amid the flames, ever in union with sus, Who remained in her soul and in that body hich was sacrificed.

rength of the Martyrs

The whole history of the martyrs, from St. ephen, the protomartyr, to the angelic martyr, St. arcisus, and the more recent martyrs, is a story of e super-human strength which the Eucharist be- ows on them as they do battle against the devil and ainst all the hellish powers that operate in the orld (cf. I Pet. 5:9).

Remember, also, the heavenly comfort and help hich Holy Communion brings to the sick, and not erely to their souls, but to their bodies also, which metimes become wonderfully healed. It used to ppen, for example, to St. Lidwina and to Alexandria a Costa, that during the whole time the Sacred ecies remained within their bodies, their terrible ysical sufferings would marvellously cease. It like- se happened to St. Lawrence of Brindisi and St. ter Claver, that all the pains of the serious ailments at had been tormenting them, would cease when ey were celebrating Holy Mass.

ke care of the soul first

But most consoling of all is the Christian's final oly Communion, which is called Viaticum; that is, od for the journey from this life to the next. Oh, hat great importance the Saints attached to our ceiving It in good time and with the best disposi- ons!

When St. Dominic Savio was sent home because of

a grave illness, the doctor held out good hopes of hi
recovery. But the holy youth called his father and
said, "Father, it will be a good thing if I deal with the
heavenly Doctor. I want to go to Confession and re
ceive Holy Communion."

When St. Anthony Claret's declining health begar
to cause serious concern, two physicians were called
in for advice. Noticing this, the Saint realized the
gravity of his illness and said, "I understand; but firs
let us think about the soul, and then the body." And
he wanted to receive the Sacraments at once. After
that was done, he sent for the two physicians and
told them, "Now do what you want to do."

First the soul, and then the body. Is it possible
that we do not appreciate this? Often we are so un
thinking that we concern ourselves a great deal abou
getting the doctor in to tend to the sick person
whereas we get around to summoning the priest only
at the last minute when the patient is, perhaps, too
far gone to receive the Sacraments with full awareness
or cannot even receive them at all. Oh how foolish
how unwise we are! How can we escape being answer
able, if, by failing to call the priest on time, we put
dying person's salvation in jeopardy and deprive him
of the support and great help that he could receive in
his last moments?

The Eucharist is the highest guarantee pledging
true life to the Christian who dwells in this poor land
of exile. "Our bodies," writes St. Gregory of Nyassa
"when united to Christ's Body, gain a beginning o
immortality, because they are united to Immortality.
When the body's short life is failing, we look to Jesus
Who is eternal Life. He is given to us in Holy Com
munion in order to be the true and enduring Life of
our immortal souls and to be the Resurrection of our
mortal bodies: "He who eats My Flesh and drinks My
Blood has life everlasting" (John 6:55). "He who eats

is Bread shall live forever" (John 6:59), because "I n the Resurrection and the Life" (John 11:25).

Ah! What a great grace Holy Viaticum is! When the oly Curé of Ars was dying and heard the ringing of e bell that announced the arrival of Holy Viaticum, e was moved to tears, and said, "How can we not eep when Jesus is coming for the last time to us th so much love?"

Yes, Jesus in the Holy Eucharist is Love that has come my food, my strength, my life, my heart's aving. Every time I receive Him, during life or at e time of death, He makes Himself mine in order to ake me His. Yes, He is all mine and I am all His - the e in the other, the one belonging to the other (cf. hn 6:57). This is the fullness of Love for the soul d for the body, on earth and in Heaven.

ery Day With Him

Jesus is in the tabernacle for my sake. He is the od of my soul. "My Flesh is food indeed and My ood is drink indeed" (John 6:56). If I want to urish myself spiritually and be fully supplied with e, I must receive Him. "Amen, amen I say to you, less you eat the Flesh of the Son of Man and drink s Blood, you shall not have life in you" (John 54). St. Augustine informs us that the Catholic ople in his diocese in Africa called the Eucharist by e word "Life." When they were to go to Holy Com- nion, they would say, "We are going to the Life." at a wonderful way of expressing it!

To keep my supernatural powers and energies - my pernatural life - in good health, I must nourish em. The Holy Eucharist is exactly what is needed this, for It is the "Bread of life" (John 6:35), the read that has come down from heaven" (John 59), which bestows, replenishes, preserves and in- ases the spiritual energies of the soul. St. Peter J.

Eymard ventured to say, "Communion is as necessary for us to sustain our Christian vitality, as the vision of God is necessary to the angels, to maintain their life of glory."

Every day I ought to nourish my soul, just as every day I feed my body in order to give it physical vitality. St. Augustine teaches, "The Eucharist is a daily Bread that we take as a remedy for the frailty we suffer from daily." And St. Peter J. Eymard adds, "Jesus has prepared not just one Host, but One for every day of our life. The Hosts for us are ready. Let us not forfeit even One of Them."

Jesus is that Host, that Victim of love, Who is so sweet and so healthful to the soul, as to move St. Gemma Galgani to say, "I feel a great need to be strengthened anew by that Food so sweet, which Jesus offers me. This affectionate therapy that Jesus gives me every morning unstiffens me and draws to Him every affection of my heart."

For the Saints, daily Communion fulfills an imperative need for Life and Love, corresponding to Jesus' divine desire to give Himself to be every soul's Life and Love. We should not forget that Holy Thursday was the day for which Jesus had "longed" (cf. Luke 22:15). Hence, the holy Curé of Ars said emphatically, "Every Consecrated Host is made to burn Itself up with love in a human heart." And St. Therese of Lisieux wrote to another Sister, "It is not in order to occupy a golden ciborium that Jesus every day comes down from heaven, but it is to find another heaven, namely, our soul, in which He takes His delight," and when a soul well able to do so does not want to receive Jesus into its heart, "Jesus weeps." "Therefore," continues St. Therese, "when the devil cannot enter with sin into a soul's sanctuary, he wants the soul to be at least unoccupied, with no Master, and well removed from Holy Communion." It should surely be evident that we are here concerned with a snare of the devil; for only the devil can be interested in keeping us away from Jesus. May we be on our guard, then. We should try not to fall victim to the devil's deceptions. "Endeavor not to miss any Holy Communion," St. Margaret Mary Alacoque advises; "We can scarcely give our enemy, the devil, greater joy than when we withdraw from Jesus, Who takes away the power the enemy has over us."

Daily Communion is a daily wellspring of love, of strength, of light, of joy, of courage, of every virtue and every good. "If anyone thirst, let him come to Me and drink," Jesus said (John 7:37). He alone is the "Fountain of water springing up unto life everlasting" (John 4:14). How can there be anyone who is in the state of Sanctifying Grace not want, or who finds it hard, to go to this divine "table of the Lord" (1 Cor. 10:21)?

The great Lord Chancellor of England, St. Thomas More, who died a martyr because of his resistance to schism, used to hear Mass every morning and receive Holy Communion. Some friends tried to persuade him that this care was not suitable for a layman heavily engaged in so many affairs of state. "You present all your reasons, and they rather convince me the more that I **should** receive Holy Communion every day," he said. "My distractions are numerous, and with Jesus I learn to recollect myself. The occasions of offending God are frequent, and I receive strength every day from Him to flee from them. I need light and prudence to manage very difficult affairs, and every day I can consult Jesus in Holy Communion. He is my great Teacher."

Someone once asked the celebrated biologist, Banting, why he cared so much about daily Communion. "Have you ever reflected," he answered, "what would happen if the dew did not fall every night? No plant could develop. The grass and flowers could not survive the evaporations and the dryness that the day's heat brings in one way or another. Their cycle of energies, their natural renewal, the balance of their lymphatic fluids, the very life of plants requires this dew..." After a pause, he continued: "Now my soul is like a little plant. It is something rather frail that the winds and heat do battle with every day. So it is necessary that every morning I go get my fresh stock of spiritual dew, by going to Holy Communion."

St. Joseph Cottolengo recommended to the physicians of his House of Divine Providence that they hear Mass and go to Communion before undertaking their difficult surgeries. This was because, as he said, "Medicine is a great science, but God is the great Physician." Blessed Joseph Moscati, the celebrated physician of Naples, used to be very regular about this, and go to unbelievable lengths (at the cost of enormous inconvenience, especially in view of the frequent trips he had to make) to avoid missing daily Communion. If on any day it was quite impossible to receive Communion, he had not the courage that day to make his doctor's calls; for he said, "Without Jesus I do not have enough light to save my poor patients."

Oh, the ardent love the Saints have for daily Holy Communion! And who can properly describe it? St. Joseph Cupertino, who did not fail to receive his beloved Lord every day, once ventured to say to his brothers in religious life, "Be sure that I will depart into the next life on the day that I cannot receive the Pecoriello (the Great Lamb)" as he affectionately and devotedly called the Divine Lamb. And, in fact, it took a severe illness to prevent him from receiving Our Lord in the Eucharist one day; and that was the day of his death!

When St. Gemma Galgani's father was worried about his daughter's health, he criticized her for setting out too early every morning to go to Mass. His criticism drew this answer from the Saint: "But Father, as for me, I become ill if I don't receive Jesus in the Holy Eucharist."

When St. Catherine of Genoa learned of the interdict put on her city, carrying a prohibition against Mass and Holy Communion, she went on foot every day to a remote Sanctuary outside Genoa in order to go to Communion. When she was told that she was overdoing things, the Saint replied, "If I had to go miles and miles over burning coals in order to receive Jesus, I would say the way was easy, as if I were walking on a carpet of roses."

This should teach a lesson to us who may have a Church within a short walk, where we can go at our convenience to receive Jesus into our hearts. And even if this should cost us some sacrifice, would it not be worth it?

But there is yet more to this, if we reflect that the Saints would have wanted to receive Communion not just once, but several times a day.

Full Ciborium, Empty Breadboxes

Let us go forward! We should not apologize for doing something so holy as receiving daily Communion, to which every blessing for soul and body is attached.

Blessings for the Soul

As for blessings for the soul, St. Cyril of Alexandria, Father and Doctor of the Church, wrote: "If the poison of pride is swelling up in you, turn to the Eucharist; and that Bread, Which is your God humbling and disguising Himself, will teach you humility. If the fever of selfish greed rages in you, feed on this

59

Bread; and you will learn generosity. If the cold wind of coveting withers you, hasten to the Bread of Angels; and charity will come to blossom in your heart. If you feel the itch of intemperance, nourish yourself with the Flesh and Blood of Christ, Who practiced heroic self-control during His earthly life; and you will become temperate. If you are lazy and sluggish about spiritual things, strengthen yourself with this heavenly Food; and you will grow fervent. Lastly, if you feel scorched by the fever of impurity, go to the banquet of the Angels; and the spotless Flesh of Christ will make you pure and chaste."

When people wanted to know how it came about that St. Charles Borromeo kept chaste and upright in the midst of other youths who were loose and frivolous, this was his secret: frequent Holy Communion. It was this same St. Charles who recommended frequent Communion to the young St. Aloysius Gonzaga, who became the Saint of angelic purity. Assuredly, the Eucharist proves to be "the wheat of the elect and wine which sprouts forth virgins" (Zach. 9:17). And St. Philip Neri, a priest thoroughly familiar with young people, remarked, "Devotion to the Blessed Sacrament and devotion to the Blessed Virgin are not simply the best way, but in fact the only way to keep purity. At the age of twenty nothing but Communion can keep one's heart pure ... Chastity is not possible without the Eucharist." This is most true.

Blessings for the Body

And what of the blessings that the Holy Eucharist brings for the body? St. Luke said of Our Lord, "Power went forth from Him and healed all" (Luke 6:19). How many times at Lourdes has this not again proved true of Our Savior in the Eucharist? How many bodies have been healed by this kind Lord, veiled within the white Host? How many people, who were suffering from sickness or from poverty, have there not been who have received, with the Eucharistic Bread, the bread of health, of strength, and aid for other needs?

One day St. Joseph Cottolengo noticed that a number of patients in his House of Providence had not chosen to receive Holy Communion. The ciborium remained full. Now that same day the pantry ran out of bread for the forthcoming meal. The Saint, setting the ciborium on the altar, turned and very animatedly made this expressive statement: "Full ciborium, empty bread boxes!"

This bore out a truth. Jesus is the fullness of life and love for my soul. Without Him, all else is empty and arid. With Him I have limitless reserves every day for every good, purity and joy.

Spiritual Communion

Spiritual Communion is the reserve of Eucharistic Life and Love always available for lovers of the Eucharistic Jesus. By means of Spiritual Communion the loving desires are satisfied of the soul that wants to be united with Jesus, its dear Bridegroom. Spiritual Communion is a union of love between the soul and Jesus in the Host. This union is spiritual but nonetheless real, more real than the union between the soul and the body, "because the soul lives more where it loves than where it lives," says St. John of the Cross.

Faith, Love and Desire

As is evident, Spiritual Communion assumes that we have faith in the Real Presence of Jesus in the Tabernacle. It implies that we would like Sacramental Communion, and it demands a gratitude for Jesus' gift of this Sacrament. All this is expressed simply and briefly in the formula of St. Alphonsus: "My Jesus, I believe that You are really present in the most Blessed Sacrament. I love Thee above all things, and I desire to possess Thee within my soul. Since I cannot now receive Thee sacramentally, come at least spiritually into my heart. - (Pause) I embrace Thee as being already there and unite myself wholly to Thee. Never, never permit me to be separated from Thee. Amen."

Spiritual Communion, as St. Thomas Aquinas and St. Alphonsus Liguori teach, produces effects similar to Sacramental Communion, according to the dispositions with which it is made, the greater or less earnestness with which Jesus is desired, and the greater or less love with which Jesus is welcomed and given due attention.

A special advantage of Spiritual Communion is that we can make it as **often** as we like - even hundreds of times a day - **when** we like - even late at night - and **wherever** we like - even in a desert, or up in an airplane.

It is fitting to make a Spiritual Communion especially when we are attending Holy Mass and cannot receive Our Lord sacramentally. While the priest is receiving his Holy Communion, our soul should share in it by inviting Jesus into our heart. In this way every Holy Mass we hear is a complete one, with the Offertory, the sacrificial Consecration, and Holy Communion.

<u>The two chalices</u>

Jesus Himself told St. Catherine of Siena in a vision how precious a Spiritual Communion is. The Saint was afraid that a Spiritual Communion was nothing compared to a Sacramental Communion. In the vision Our Lord held up two ciboriums, and said, "In this golden ciborium I put your Sacramental Communions. In this silver ciborium I put your Spiritual Communions. Both ciboriums are quite pleasing to Me."

The surest means of remaining immune to the pestiferous disease that surrounds us is to fortify ourselves with Eucharistic food.   **Padre Pio**

And once Jesus said to St. Margaret Mary Alacoque when she was absorbed in addressing yearning sighs to Him in the tabernacle, "I love so much a soul's desire to receive Me, that I hasten to it each time it summons Me by its yearnings."

It is not hard to see how much Spiritual Communion has been loved by the Saints. Spiritual Communion at least partly satisfied that ardent desire to be united to their Beloved. Jesus Himself said, "Abide in Me and I in you" (John 15:4). And Spiritual Communion helps us stay united to Jesus, even when we are far from a Church. There was no other way to appease the fond yearning that burned in the hearts of the Saints. "O God, my whole soul longs for You. As a deer for running water, my whole soul thirsts for God" (Ps. 41:2).

This is the loving sigh of the Saints. St. Catherine of Genoa exclaimed, "O dear Spouse (of my soul), I so strongly crave the joy of being with Thee, that it seems to me that if I were dead, I would come to life in order to receive Thee in Holy Communion." Blessed Agatha of the Cross felt such an acute yearning to live always united to Jesus in the Eucharist that she remarked, "If the Confessor had not taught me to make Spiritual Communion, I could not have lived."

For St. Mary Frances of the Five Wounds, likewise, Spiritual Communion was the only relief from the acute pain she felt when shut up at home far from her beloved Lord, especially when she was not allowed to receive Sacramental Communion. At such a time she went out on the terrace of her home and, looking at the Church, she tearfully sighed, "Happy are they who have received Thee today in the Blessed Sacrament, O Jesus. Blessed are the walls of the Church that guard my Jesus. Blessed are the priests, who are ways near the most lovable Jesus." Spiritual Communion alone was able to satisfy her a little.

During the day

Here is one of the counsels which Padre Pio of Pietrelcina gave to one of his spiritual daughters: "In the course of the day, when it is not permitted to you to do otherwsie, call Jesus, even in the midst of all your occupations, with a resigned sigh of the soul and He will come and will remain always united with your soul by means of His grace and His holy love. Make a spiritual flight before the Tabernacle, when you cannot go there with your body, and there pour out the ardent desires of your spirit and embrace the beloved of souls, better than if it had been permitted to you to receive Him sacramentally."

Let us, too, profit by this great gift. During the times that we suffer trial or feel abandoned, for example, what can be more valuable to us than the company of our Sacramental Lord by means of spiritual Communion? This holy practice can work with ease to fill our days with acts and sentiments of love, and can make us live in an embrace of love that depends just on our often renewing it so that we scarcely ever interrupt it.

St. Angela Merici was extremely fond of Spiritual Communion. Not only did she make it often and exhort others to do it, but she chose to leave it as an inheritance to her daughters, so that they might practice it ever afterwards.

What shall we say of St. Francis de Sales? Does not his whole life seem like a chain of Spiritual Communions? He made a resolution to make a Spiritual Communion at least every quarter of an hour. Saint Maximilian M. Kolbe had the same resolve from the time of his youth. The Servant of God, Andrew Baltrami, has left us a short page of his personal diary, which is a little program for a life lived in uninterrupted Spiritual Communion with Jesus in the Blessed Sacrament. These are his words: "Wherever I may be I will often think of Jesus in the Blessed Sacrament. I will fix my thoughts on the holy Tabernacle - even when I happen to wake up at night - adoring Him from where I am, calling to Jesus in the Blessed Sacrament, offering up to Him the action I am performing. I will install one telegraph cable from my study to the Church, another from my bedroom, and a third from our refectory; and as often as I can, I will send messages of love to Jesus in the Blessed Sacrament." What a stream of divine affections must have passed over those precious cables!

Also during the night

The Saints were eager to make use of these and similar holy means in order to find an outlet for their overflowing hearts; for they never felt they had gone far enough in their endeavor to love. "The more I love Thee, the less I love Thee," exclaimed St. Frances Xavier Cabrini, "because I would like to love Thee more, but I cannot. Oh enlarge, enlarge my heart."

When St. Roch spent five years in prison because he had been judged to be a dangerous vagabond, in his cell he kept his eyes ever fixed at the window praying in the meantime. The guard asked, "What are you looking at?" The Saint answered, "I am looking at the tower of the parish church." The tower reminded him of a church, a tabernacle, and the Eucharistic Jesus, inseparably joined to his heart.

The holy Cure of Ars said to his flock, "At the sight of a church tower you can say: Jesus is there, for there a priest has celebrated Mass." Blessed Louis Guanella, when he was travelling by train with pilgrimages to the various shrines, used to always advise pilgrims to turn their minds and hearts to esus every time they saw a church tower from the arriage window, "Every bell tower," he would say, indicates a church, where there is a Tabernacle, where Mass is said, and where Jesus stays."

Let us take a lesson from the Saints. They would ke to pass on some spark of the love burning in their earts. Let us undertake to make many Spiritual Communions, especially during the busiest moments of he day. Then soon the fire of love will enter us. For omething very consoling that St. Leonard of Port Maurice assures us of, is this: "If you practice the oly exercise of Spiritual Communion a good many imes each day, within a month you will see yourself ompletely changed." Hardly a month - clear enough, s it not?

"*My heart feels as if it were being drawn by a superior force each morning just before uniting with Him in the Blessed Sacrament. I have such a thirst and hunger before receiving Him that it's a wonder I don't die of anxiety. I was hardly able to reach the Divine Prisoner in order to celebrate Mass. When Mass ended I remained with Jesus to render Him thanks. My thirst and hunger do not diminish after I have received Him in the Blessed Sacrament, but rather, increase steadily. Oh, how sweet was the conversation I held with Paradise this morning. The heart of Jesus and my own, if you will pardon the expression, fused. They were no longer two hearts beating but only one. My heart disappeared as if it were a drop in the ocean.*"

Padre Pio

"I am with you all days, even to the consummation of the world" (Matt. 28:20).

Chapter Four
JESUS WITH ME

- The Real Presence
- Visits to Jesus
- Jesus I Adore Thee!
- Loving Jesus' House

"In Holy Communion Jesus gives Himself to me and becomes mine, all mine, in His Body, Blood, Soul and Divinity."
- Father Stephano Manelli

The Real Presence

The Real Presence of Jesus in our tabernacles is God's mystery, God's Gift, God's Love. During the Holy Mass at the time of the Consecration, when the priest pronounces Jesus' divine words, "This is My Body ... This is the chalice of My Blood" (Matt. 26: 26-27), the bread and wine become the Body and Blood of Jesus. The substance of the bread and of the wine are no longer there, because they have been transformed - "transubstantiated" - into the divine Body and Blood of Jesus. The bread and wine keep only their appearances, to express the reality of food and drink, according to Jesus' words, "My Flesh is real food and My Blood is real drink" (John 6:56).

Behind the veil, the disguise, of the Host, and within the Chalice, there is the Divine Person of Jesus with His Body, Blood, Soul, and Divinity. This is what is given to whoever receives Holy Communion, and is what continually remains in the consecrated Hosts placed in the tabernacle.

St. Ambrose wrote: "How is the change of bread into the Body of Christ brought about? It is by means of the Consecration. With what words is the Consecration accomplished? It is with the words of Jesus. When the moment arrives for accomplishing this sacred wonder, the priest ceases to speak as himself; he speaks in the person of Jesus."

The words of Consecration are the most wonderful and awesome words that God has given to the Church. They have the power, through the priest, to transform a bit of bread and wine into our crucified God, Jesus! They achieve this wonderful, mysterious feat by a supreme power which surpasses the power of the Seraphim and belongs only to God and to His priests. We should not wonder that there have been holy priests who suffered a great deal when they pronounced those divine words. St. Joseph of Copertino, and in our time, Padre Pio of Pietrelcina, appeared visibly weighed down with distress, and they managed only with difficulty and with pauses to complete the two formulas of Consecration.

The Father Guardian ventured to ask St. Joseph of Copertino, "How is it you recite the whole Mass so well, and stammer at each syllable of the Consecration?"

The Saint answered, "The sacred words of the Consecration are like burning coals on my lips. When I pronounce them, I have to do it like one who has to swallow boiling hot food."

It is through these divine words of Consecration that Jesus is on our altars, in our tabernacles, and in the Hosts. But how is it that all this comes about?

"How is it possible," an educated Mohammedan asked a missionary bishop, "that bread and wine should become the Flesh and Blood of Christ?"

The bishop answered, "You were small when you were born. You grew big because your body changed the food you took into flesh and blood. If a man's body is able to transform bread and wine into flesh and blood, then God can do it far more easily."

The Mohammedan then asked: "How is it possible for Jesus to be wholly and entirely present in a little Host?"

The bishop answered, "Look at the landscape before you and consider how much smaller your eye is in comparison to it. Now within your little eye there is an image of this vast countryside. Can God not do in reality, in His Person, what is done in us by way of a likeness or image?"

Then the Mohammedan asked, "How is it possible for the same Body to be present at the same time in all your churches and in all the consecrated Hosts?

The bishop said, "Nothing is impossible with God - and this answer ought to be enough. But nature also answers this question. Let us take a mirror, throw it down on the floor and let it break into pieces. Every piece can carry the same image that the whole mirror formerly reproduced. Likewise, the self-same Jesus reproduces Himself, not as a mere likeness, but as a reality, in every consecrated Host. He is truly present in each One of Them."

Eucharistic wonders are recorded in the lives of St. Rose of Lima, Blessed Angela of Foligno, St. Catherine of Siena, St. Philip Neri, St. Francis Borgia, St. Joseph of Copertino, and many other Saints, whose senses perceived the Real Presence of Jesus in the tabernacle and in the consecrated Hosts, as they saw Jesus with their own eyes or experienced His ineffable fragrance. We have also accounts of how St. Anthony of Padua once proved to an unbeliever the Real Presence by showing him a hungry mule kneeling before a monstrance containing the Blessed Sacrament, in preference to devouring the basket of oats placed beside the monstrance. Also remarkable was an episode concerning St. Alphonsus M. Liguori when he received Holy Communion in his sickbed. One morning, as soon as he had received the host, he sighed aloud with tears, "What have you done: You have brought me a host without Jesus - an unconsecrated host!" The matter was investigated and it was learned that the priest who had said the Mass that morning had been so distracted that he had left out everything from the Memento for the Living to the Memento for the Dead in the Roman Canon, and had thereby completely omitted the consecration of the bread and wine. The Saint had detected the absence of Our Lord from the unconsecrated host!

Many other episodes taken from the lives of saints could be mentioned. Likewise, instances of exorcism could be told where obsessed persons were delivered from the demon by means of the Eucharist. Also, one could cite those great witnesses of faith and love which are the Eucharistic Congresses and the celebrated Eucharistic shrines (such as those at Turin, Lanciano[1], Siena, Orvieto, and the shrine of St. Peter of Patierno), shrines that even today offer worthy up-to-date testimony of astonishing events of the past confirming the Real Presence.

But outweighing all these factual histories and evidences, is the faith by which the truth of the Real Presence is assured and on which we must base our unwavering certainty that it is the truth. "Jesus is the Truth" (John 14:6), and He has left us the Eucharist as a mystery of faith for us to believe with our whole mind and our whole heart.

When the Angelic Doctor, St. Thomas Aquinas, was brought Holy Viaticum, he rose up out of the ashes where he had been laid, got on his knees, and said, "I would not believe with greater assurance that He Whom I am to receive is the Son of the Eternal God, even if I had a clear enlightenment about it a thousand times clearer than that of faith."

Mysterium fidei (Mystery of faith)

With these words Pope Paul VI chose to caption his encyclical on the Eucharist, simply because the divine realities have no source of truth and of certainty that ranks higher than theological faith. It was due to this faith that Saints merited to see Jesus the Host, though they had wanted no further proof than what they had; namely, God's word. Pope Gregory XV declared that St. Teresa of Jesus (whom he canonized) "saw Our Lord Jesus Christ, present in the Host so distinctly with the eyes of her spirit that she said she did not begrudge the happy lot of

[1] See the supplement on page 126 of this book.

he Blessed who behold the Lord face to face in eaven." And St. Dominic Savio once wrote in his ary, "I need nothing in this world in order to be appy. I only need to see Jesus in heaven, Whom I ow see and adore on the altar with the eyes of ith."

It is with this faith that we ought to approach the oly Eucharist and keep ourselves in that divine resence, loving Jesus in this Sacrament and making thers love Him.

adre Pio was delighted when they brought him young children who were repared for First Holy Communion. Father Manelli, the author of "Jesus, ur Eucharistic Love" went to first Confession and First Communion to adre Pio at about the age of five.

Visits to Jesus

Jesus is in our tabernacles, and this fact we call th[e] Real Presence. The same Jesus Who was sheltered b[y] Mary Immaculate within her virginal body, is in th[e] little body of a white Host. The same Jesus Who wa[s] whipped, crowned with thorns, and crucified as [a] Victim for the sins of the world, remains in the cib[o]rium in the Host as a Victim sacrificed for our salv[a]tion. The same Jesus Who rose from the dead an[d] ascended into Heaven, where He now is glorious[ly] reigning at the right hand of the Father, resides o[n] our altars, surrounded by a multitude of countle[ss] adoring Angels - a sight that Blessed Angela of Foli[g]no beheld in a vision.

Thus Jesus is truly with us. "Jesus is there!" - Th[e] holy Cure of Ars could not finish repeating thes[e] three words without shedding tears. And St. Pete[r] Julian Eymard exclaimed with joyful fervor, "Ther[e] Jesus is! Therefore all of us should go visit Him[!] And when St. Teresa of Jesus heard someone sa[y] "If only I had lived at the time of Jesus ... If only [I] had seen Jesus ... If only I had talked with Jesus ...[,] she responded in her spirited way, "But do we n[ot] have in the Eucharist the living, true and real Jes[us] present before us? Why look for more?"

The Saints certainly did not seek for more. The[y] knew where Jesus was, and they desired no mo[re] than the privilege of keeping inseparable compan[y] with Him, both in their affections, and by bodi[ly] presence. Being ever with our beloved - is this not on[e] of the primary things true love calls for? Indeed it i[s] and, therefore, we know that visits to the Blesse[d] Sacrament and the Eucharistic Benediction were t[he] secret yet evident loves of the Saints. The time [of] paying a visit to Jesus is wholly the time of love - [a] love we will resume practising in Paradise, sin[ce] ove alone "does not come to an end" (I Cor. 13:8). St. Catherine of Genoa made no blunder in saying, "The time I have spent before the tabernacle is the best spent time of my life."

Let us see some examples from the Saints.

Saint Maximilian M. Kolbe, apostle of the Immaculate Virgin, used to make an average of ten visits a day to the Blessed Sacrament - a practice he began as a young student. During the school year, during the intervals between classes, he would hasten to the chapel so that in the mornings he managed to make five visits to Jesus. During the rest of the day he made five more visits. Among these, one was what he considered always a compulsory stop during the afternoon walk. It was in a church (in Rome) where the Blessed Sacrament was exposed.

Also, St. Robert Bellarmine during his youth, when on his way to and from school, used to pass a church four times. Thus, four times a day he would stop and pay a visit to Jesus.

How often does it happen that we pass by a church? Are we perhaps rather thoughtless and callous? The Saints hoped they would meet a church along the road they were taking; whereas, we are quite indifferent, even if we find churches before us. Ven. J.J. Olier wrote: "When there are two routes to get me to a certain place, I take the one on which I meet more churches, in order to be nearer the Blessed Sacrament. When I see a place where my Jesus is, I am so happy, and I say, 'You are here, my God and my All.' "

St. Alphonsus Rodrigues was a door-keeper. His duties often took him by the chapel door; and then

he would never fail to at least look in to give Our
Lord a loving glance. When he left the house and
when he returned, he always visited Jesus to ask His
blessing.

The angelic youth, St. Stanislaus Kostka, took
advantage of every free moment to hurry off to visit
Jesus in the Blessed Sacrament. When he simply could
not make it, he would turn to his Guardian Angel and
tell him quietly, "My dear Angel, go there for me."
And what a truly angelic assignment! Why can we
not make such a request? Our Guardian Angel would
be quite glad to comply. In fact, we could not ask
him to do us a nobler and more agreeable favour.

St. Augustine has left us an account about his
mother, St. Monica, which tells how, every day, be-
sides attending Mass, she went twice to visit Our
Lord, once in the morning and once in the evening.
Another holy mother of seven children used to do
the same, Blessed Anna Maria Taigi. And St. Wenceslaus, King of Bohemia, used to make frequent trips
day and night, even in the rigors of winter, to visit
the Blessed Sacrament in churches.

Here is another happy example in a royal famliy.
When St. Elizabeth of Hungary was a little girl and
used to play about the palace with her companions,
she would always pick a spot near the chapel so that
every now and then, without being noticed, she
might stop by the chapel door, kiss the lock, and
say to Jesus, "My Jesus, I am playing, but I am not
forgetting You. Bless me and my companions. I will
see You again." What simple devotion!

Francisco, one of the three little shepherds of
Fatima, was a little contemplative, and he had an
ardent love for visiting the Blessed Sacrament. He

wanted to go often and stay in church as long as he could in order to be near the tabernacle close to the "hidden Jesus," as he called the Eucharist in his childlike, profound way of speaking. When sickness confined him to bed, he confided to his cousin, Lucy, that his greatest pain was not being able to go visit the "hidden Jesus" to take Him all his kisses and his love. Here we have a little boy teaching us how to love!

We may add that St. Francis Borgia used to make at least seven visits to the Blessed Sacrament every day. St. Mary Magdalene de Pazzi was making thirty-three visits a day during one period of her life. Blessed Mary Fortunata Viti, a humble Benedictine nun of our times, used to do the same. Blessed Agatha of the Cross, a Dominican tertiary, succeeded in making a hundred visits a day, going from her residence to a church. Finally, what shall we say of Alexandria da Costa, who, when bed-ridden for many years, was continually making flights in her heart to visit all the "Holy Tabernacles" in the world?

Perhaps these examples astonish us and might seem to us exceptional, even among Saints. But that is not the case. Visits to the Blessed Sacrament are acts of faith and love. Whoever has the greater faith and love, feels more strongly the need of being with Jesus. And what did the Saints live by if not by faith and love?

One day a resourceful catechist said to his young pupils, "If an angel were to come to you from heaven and tell you, 'Jesus in person is in such and such a house and is waiting for you,' would you not at once leave everything in order to hasten to Him? You would interrupt any amusement or anything that occupied you; you would count yourself fortunate to be able to make a little sacrifice in order to go and be with Jesus. Now be sure, and do not forget, that Jesus is in the tabernacle, and He is **always waiting** for you, because He wants to have you near and desires to greatly enrich you with His graces."

How greatly, how highly, have the Saints valued the physical presence of Jesus in person in the tabernacle and Jesus' desire to have us near Him? So greatly, so highly, as to make St. Francis de Sales say, "We must visit Jesus in the Blessed Sacrament a hundred thousand times a day."

Let us learn from the Saints to love our visits to Jesus in the Eucharist. Let us make these visits. Let us linger with Him, talking with Him affectionately about what is in our heart. He will fondly look upon us and draw us to His Heart. "When we speak to Jesus with simplicity and with all our heart," said the holy Curé of Ars, "He does like a mother who holds her child's head with her hands and covers it with kisses, and caresses."

If we do not know how to make visits to the tabernacle which include heart-to-heart talks, we should obtain the beautiful, matchless booklet of St. Alphonsus entitled **Visits to the Blessed Sacrament and to the Blessed Virgin Mary**. Something unforgettable is the way Padre Pio of Pietrelcina, every evening, used to read with a tearful voice one of St. Alphonsus' **Visits** during the Exposition of the Blessed Sacrament just before the Eucharistic Benediction.

Let us get started and be faithful in making at least one visit a day to Our Lord Who is fondly waiting. Then let us try to increase these visits according to our ability. And, if we have no time to make long visits, let us make "stop-ins," that is, let us enter the church every time we can and kneel down for a few moments before the Blessed Sacrament, saying affectionately, "Jesus, Thou art here. I adore Thee. I love Thee. Come into my heart." This is something simple and short, but, oh, so profitable! Let us always remember these consoling words of St. Alphonsus: "You may be sure that of all the moments of your life, the time you spend before the divine Sacrament will be that which will give you more strength during life and more consolation at the hour of your death and during eternity."

JESUS, I ADORE THEE!

When there is true love, and it mounts to a certain point, there is adoration. Great love and adoration are two distinct things; but, they form one whole. They become adoring love and loving adoration.

Jesus in the tabernacle is adored only by those who truly love Him, and He is loved in the highest manner by whoever adores Him.

The Saints, being far advanced in the practice of love, were faithful and ardent adorers of Jesus in the Blessed Sacrament. Importantly, Eucharistic adoration has always been considered as the closest likeness we have to the eternal adoration which will make up our whole paradise. The difference lies only in the veil which hides the sight of that divine Reality of which faith gives us unwavering certainty.

Adoration of the Blessed Sacrament has been the fervent devotion of the Saints. Their adoration lasted hours and hours, sometimes whole days or nights. There "at Jesus' feet" like Mary of Bethany (Luke 10:39), keeping Him fond and intimate company, absorbed in contemplating Him, they surrendered their hearts in a pure and fragrant offering of adoring love. Hear what Brother Charles de Foucauld wrote before the tabernacle: "What a tremendous delight, my God! To spend over fifteen hours without anything else to do but look at You and tell You, 'Lord, I love You!' Oh, what sweet delight!"

All the Saints have been ardent adorers of the Holy Eucharist, from the great Doctors of the Church like St. Thomas Aquinas and St. Bonaventure, to Popes like St. Pius V and St. Pius X, priests like the holy Curé of Ars and St. Peter Julian Eymard, down to humble souls like St. Rita, St. Paschal Baylon, St. Bernadette Soubirous, St. Gerard, St. Dominic Savio and St. Gemma Galgani. These chosen ones, whose love was true, kept no count of the hours of fond adoration that they spent day and night before Jesus in the tabernacle.

Consider how St. Francis of Assisi spent so much time, often entire nights, before the altar, and remained there so devoutly and humbly that he deeply moved anyone who stopped to watch him. Consider how St. Benedict Labre, called the "Poor man of the Forty Hours", spent days in churches in which the Blessed Sacrament was solemnly exposed. For years and years this Saint was seen in Rome making pilgrimages from church to church where the Forty Hours was being held, and remaining there before Jesus always on his knees absorbed in adoring prayer motionless for eight hours, even when his friends, the insects, were crawling on him and stinging him all over.

When someone wanted to do a portrait of St Aloysius Gonzaga, there was a discussion about what posture to give him. The decision reached was to portray the saint in adoration before the altar, because Eucharistic adoration was characteristic of him and was most expressive of his holiness.

That favorite of the Sacred Heart, St. Margaret Mary Alacoque, on one Holy Thursday, spent fourteen hours without interruption prostrate in adora ion. St. Frances Xavier Cabrini, on a feast of the Sacred Heart, remained in adoration twelve continuous hours. She had been so absorbed and attentive to Our Lord in the Eucharist that when a Sister asked her if she had liked the arrangement of flowers and draping that adorned the altar, she answered, "I did not notice. I only saw one Flower, Jesus, no other."

After visiting the cathedral in Milan, St. Francis de Sales heard someone ask him, "Your Excellency, did you see what a wealth of marble there is, and how majestic the lines are?" The holy bishop answered, "What do you want me to tell you? Jesus' presence in the tabernacle has my spirit so absorbed, that all the beautiful architecture escapes my notice." What a lesson this reply is for us who go unthinkingly to visit celebrated churches as though they were museums!

Maximum Recollection

As an example of the spirit of recollection during Eucharistic adoration, Blessed Contardo Ferrini, professor at the University of Modena, had a striking experience. One day, after he entered a church to visit Our Lord, he became so absorbed in adoration, with eyes fixed on the tabernacle, that he took no notice when someone robbed him of the mantle spread over his shoulders.

"Not even a bolt of lightning could distract her," it was said of St. Mary Magdalene Postel, because she appeared so recollected and devout when adoring the Blessed Sacrament. On the other hand, once, during adoration, St. Catherine of Siena happened to raise her eyes toward a person passing by. Because of this distraction of an instant the Saint was so afflicted that she wept for some time, exclaiming, "I am a sinner! I am a sinner!"

How is it that we are not ashamed of our behaviour in church? Even before Our Lord solemnly exposed we so easily turn about to look to the right and left, and are moved and distracted by any trifle, without - and this is what is sad - without feeling any regret. Ah! The delicate, sensitive love of the Saints! St. Teresa taught that "in the presence of Jesus in the Holy Sacrament we ought to be like the Blessed in heaven before the Divine Essence." That is the way the Saints have behaved in church. The holy Cure of Ars used to adore Jesus in the Blessed Sacrament with such fervor and recollection that people became convinced he saw Jesus in person with his own eyes. People said the same of St. Vincent de Paul: "He sees Jesus there within (the tabernacle)." And they said the same of St. Peter Julian Eymard, the unmatched apostle of Eucharistic adoration. Padre Pio of Pietrelcina, seeking to imitate him, was enrolled into his society of priest-adorers and for forty years kept a little image of St. Eymard on his desk.

Even After Death

It is noteworthy that the Lord seems to have favored certain Saints in singular fashion by enabling them to perform, after death, an act of adoration to the Blessed Sacrament. Thus, when St. Catherine of Bologna was placed before the Blessed Sacrament altar a few days after her death, her body rose up to a position of prayerful adoration. During the funeral Mass of St. Paschal Baylon, his eyes opened twice - at the elevation of the Host and at the elevation of the Chalice - to express his adoration of the Eucharist. When Blessed Matthew of Girgenti's body was in the church for his funeral Mass, his hands joined in adoration toward the Eucharist. At Ravello, Blessed Bonaventure of Potenza's body, while being carried past the altar of the Blessed Sacrament, made devout head-bow to Jesus in the tabernacle.

It is really true that "Love is stronger than death" (Cant.8:6), and that "He that eateth this Bread shall live forever" (John 6:59). The Eucharist is Jesus our Love. The Eucharist is Jesus our Life. Adoration of the Blessed Sacrament is a heavenly love which enlivens us and makes us one with Jesus Victim, who "incessantly intercedes for us" (Heb. 7:25). We should be mindful that one who adores, makes himself one with Jesus in the Host as Jesus intercedes with the Father for the salvation of the brethren. The highest charity toward all men is to obtain for them the kingdom of heaven. And only in Paradise will we see how many souls have been delivered from the gates of hell by the Eucharistic adoration done in reparation by holy persons known and unknown. We must not forget that at Fatima the Angel personally taught the three shepherd children the beautiful Eucharistic prayer of reparation, which we ought to learn: "O most holy Trinity, Father, Son, and Holy Spirit, I adore You profoundly, and I offer You the most precious Body, Blood, Soul and Divinity of Jesus Christ, present in all the tabernacles of the world, in reparation for the outrages, sacrileges and indifference with which He is offended. And through the infinite merits of His most Sacred Heart and of the Immaculate Heart of Mary, I beg of You the conversion of poor sinners." Eucharistic adoration is an ecstasy of love and it is the most powerful salvific practice in the apostolate of saving souls.

For this reason Saint Maximilian M. Kolbe, the great apostle of Mary, in each of his foundations, before providing even the cells of the friars, he wanted to provide the chapel in order to introduce at once perpetual adoration of the Blessed Sacrament exposed. Once, when he was taking a visitor on a tour of his "City of the Immaculate Virgin" in Poland and they had entered the large "Chapel of Adoration," with a gesture toward the Blessed Sacrament he said to his guest, "Our whole life depends on this."

The Better Part

The stigmatized friar of Gargano, to whom crowds flocked from every quarter, Padre Pio of Pietrelcina, after his long daily chore in the confessional, used to spend almost all the remaining day and night before the tabernacle in adoration, keeping company with the Madonna as he recited hundreds of Rosaries. Once the Bishop of Manfredonia, Msgr. Cesarano chose Padre Pio's friary for making an eight-day retreat. Each night the bishop got up at various times to go to the chapel, and each night at all these hours he always found Padre Pio in adoration. The great apostle of Gargano was doing his work, unseen throughout the world - and sometimes he was seen in instances of bilocation - while he remained there prostrate before Jesus, with his Rosary in his hands. He used to tell his spiritual children, "When you want to find me, come near the tabernacle."

Don James Alberione, another great apostle of our time, as a basis for his whole vast project, The Apostolate of the Press - "Societa Apostolata Stampa" expressly provided adoration of the Holy Eucharist for the Sisters in his Congregation of Pious Disciples of the Divine Master, who had the unique and specific vocation to adore Our Lord solemnly exposed in the Holy Eucharist night and day.

Eucharistic Adoration is truly that "best part" of which Jesus spoke when chiding Martha for busying herself with "many things" that were secondary overlooking the "one thing necessary" chosen by Mary, which was humble and affectionate adoration (Luke 10:41 - 42).

What should be the love and zeal, then, that we ought to have for Eucharistic adoration? If it is by

Jesus that "all things subsist" (Col. 1:17), then, to go to Him, to stay beside him, to unite ourselves with Him, means to find, to gain, to possess that whereby we and the whole universe exist. "Jesus alone is all; anything else is nothing," said St. Therese of Lisieux. To renounce, then, what is nothing for the sake of what is All, to consume our every resource and ourselves for the sake of Him Who is All, instead of for what is nothing - is this not indeed our true wealth and supreme wisdom? This was evidently the thinking of Padre Pio of Pietrelcina when he wrote, "A thousand years of enjoying human glory is not worth even an hour spent in sweetly communing with Jesus in the Blessed Sacrament."

What good reason we have to envy the Angels, as the Saints have done, because Angels ceaselessly remain stationed around the tabernacles!

Francisco Marto, as he was taught by Our Lady of Fatima, often knelt in prayer in front of the Blessed Sacrament to console Our Lord.

LOVING JESUS' HOUSE

The real presence of our Divine Lord in our tabernacles has always been something immensely reverenced and respected by the Saints. Their loving care, so artless and pure, for the "things that belong to the Lord" (I Cor. 7:32) has been one of the most obvious indications of their great love that does not hold back anything, that considers everything to be of great importance, even a simple matter of the prescribed ceremonies, for which St. Teresa and St Alphonsus declared themselves ready to sacrifice their lives.

Holiness and Decorum

And it is from the Saints that we must learn to love Jesus, surrounding with affectionate care the holy tabernacles, the altars and the churches, His "dwelling place" (Mark 11:17). Everything must express decorum, everything must inspire devotion and adoration, even in the little things, even in details. Nothing will ever be too much when it concerns loving and honoring the "King of Glory" (Psalm 23:10). One thinks of a few old practices, for example, requiring that even perfumed water be used for the ablution of the fingers of the priest during Holy Mass.

Furthermore, Jesus chose to institute the Sacrament of Love in a respectable, beautiful place, namely, the Cenacle, which was a large dining hall with furniture and carpeting (Luke 22:12). The Saints have always shown whole-hearted zeal and resourcefulness in seeing to the beauty and tidiness of the house of God.

For example, during his apostolic travels, St Francis of Assisi used to carry with him, or obtain a broom to sweep the churches he found dirty. After preaching to the people, he used to address the clergy of the town and fervently urge them to be zealous for the worthy appearance of the Lord's house. He had St. Clare and the Poor Clare Sisters prepare sacred linens for altars. In spite of his poverty, he used to obtain and send ciboria, chalices and altar cloths to poor, neglected churches.

We learn from the life of St. John Baptist de la Salle that that Saint wanted to see the chapel always clean and duly furnished, with the altar in perfect order and the sanctuary lamp always burning. Torn vestments and tarnished vessels were to him heartbreaking eyesores. He did not consider any expense too much when it came to providing for due worship of Our Lord.

St. Paul of the Cross wanted altar furnishings to be spotless. One day he sent back two corporals, one after the other, because he did not judge them to be clean enough.

Prominent among the kings who have loved the Eucharist is St. Wenceslaus, King of Bohemia. With his own hands he tilled the soil, sowed the wheat, harvested it, ground it, and sifted it. Then with the purest flour he made hosts for the Holy Sacrifice. And St. Radgundes, Queen of France, after she had become a humble religious, was happy to be able to grind with her own hands, the wheat chosen for hosts for Holy Mass, and she used to give them free to poor churches. Also noteworthy is St. Vincentia Gerosa, who took care of grapevines that supplied wine for Holy Mass. She cultivated and pruned them with her own hands, finding joy in the thought that these clusters that she had grown would become the Blood of Jesus.

What shall we say of the delicate conscience that the Saints had regarding the Blessed Sacrament?

They had uncompromising faith in the *Real Presence* of Our Lord in even the smallest visible fragment of a Host. With regard to this it is sufficient to have seen Padre Pio to see the conscientious care with which he purified the paten and the sacred vessels when he was at the altar. One could read the adoration on his face!

Once when St. Therese of Lisieux saw a small Particle of a Host on the paten after Holy Mass, she called the novices, and then carried the paten in procession into the sacristy with gracious, adoring comportment that was truly angelic. When St. Teresa Margaret found a Fragment of a Host on the floor near the altar, she broke into tears because she thought about the irreverence that might be shown to Jesus; and she knelt in adoration before the Particle until a priest came to take It and put It in the tabernacle.

Once when St. Charles Borromeo was distributing Holy Communion, he inadvertently dropped a Sacred Particle from his hand. The Saint considered himself guilty of grave irreverence to Jesus, and was so afflicted that for four days he had not the courage to celebrate Holy Mass, and as a penance he imposed an eight-day fast on himself!

What shall we say of St. Francis Xavier who at times when distributing Holy Communion felt so carried away by a sense of adoration toward Our Lord Who was in his hands, that he got on his knees and in that position continued giving Holy Communion. Did that not present a witness of faith and love worthy of heaven?

Something else even more beautiful has been the thoughtful care of the Saints who were priests, in handling the Blessed Sacrament. Oh, how they would have liked to have the same virginal hands as the Immaculate Madonna! Something noteworthy regarding St. Conrad of Costanza was that his index fingers and thumbs used to shine at night on account of the faith and the love with which he used those fingers when holding the Most Sacred Body of Jesus. St. Joseph of Copertino, an angelic Saint renowned for his ecstasies and levitations, disclosed the refined manner of his devotion when he expressed a wish to have another pair of index fingers and thumbs so that they could be used solely for holding Jesus' Most Holy Flesh. At times Padre Pio of Pietrelcina used to pick up the Sacred Host with his fingers with obvious difficulty, judging himself unworthy to allow his hands, which bore the stigmata, to have contact with the Host. (What shall we say of the painful levity with which attempts are made to introduce everywhere Communion in the hand instead of on the tongue? By comparison with the Saints - so humble, so angelic - do these people not easily present an image of presumptuous ruffians?)

Modesty of the Women

Another great concern of the Saints for the decorum of the church and for the salvation of souls, has been that of requiring modesty and decency of the women. A strict insistence on this particular point is constantly reaffirmed by all the Saints, from the Apostle, St. Paul (telling the woman to wear a veil so that her head will not be "as if she were shaven" (I Cor. 11: -6), to St. John Chrysostom, St. Ambrose, etc., down to Padre Pio of Pietrelcina, who would admit to halfway measures, but always insisted on modest dresses clearly below the knees. And how could it be otherwise? Saint Leopold da Castelnuovo used to chase women out of church who were immodestly dressed, calling them "carne da mercato ("flesh for sale"). What would he say today, when so many

women are doing away with modesty and decency
even in church? They are carrying on, even in sacred
places, the old diabolical art of seducing men to lust
of which the Holy Spirit warns us (Ecclus. 9:9). But
God's justice will not let such great madness and de-
pravity go unpunished. On the contrary, Saint Paul
says, "for which things, the wrath of God is un-
leashed" (Col. 3:6). He is referring to sins of the
flesh.

Likewise the Saints have always bidden us, by
example and by word, to follow the beautiful
practice on entering a church, of making the sign of
the cross devoutly with holy water, genuflecting
reverently, and before all else adoring Jesus in the
Blessed Sacrament in company with the angels and
Saints who keep watch around the altar. If we stop
for prayer, we need to recollect ourselves with care
to keep ourselves devout and attentive.

It is also well to draw as near as we can (observing
fitting limits) to the altar of the Blessed Sacrament
for Blessed John Duns Scotus demonstrated that the
physical influence of Jesus' Most Holy Humanity is
more intense, the closer one is to His Body and
Blood. (St. Gemma Galgani said that sometimes she
could not draw nearer the Blessed Sacrament altar
because such a fire of love burned in her heart that it
would burn the clothing over her breast!)

Whoever saw St. Francis de Sales enter a church,
bless himself, genuflect, and pray before the tabernacle, was obliged to put stock in the saying of the
people that "that is the way the Angels and Saints do
it in Heaven."

Once a prince in his Scottish court told a friend,
"If you want to see how the Angels in heaven pray,
go to church and watch how Queen Margaret prays
with her children before the altar." All hasty and

distracted people ought to give serious reflection to these words of Blessed Louis Guanella: "We may never make the church into a hallway, or a courtyard or a highway, or a public square." And St. Vincent de Paul sadly urged people that before the Blessed Sacrament they avoid making genuflections resembling the movements of marionette dolls.

May these examples and teachings of the Saints not prove fruitless for us.

We find in the Gospel a brief narrative which tells of a devoted act of love conspicuous for tastefulness and charm. It is the deed performed by St. Mary Magdalene in the house at Bethany, when she came to Jesus with "an alabaster box of precious ointment and poured it on His head" (Mt. 26:7). To provide our holy tabernacles with a setting of tastefulness and charm is a task we have always entrusted to those attractive, fragrant creatures which are flowers. In this use of them the Saints have been second to none. When the Archbishop of Turin one day chose to drop in for a visit in the Church of the Little House of Providence, he found it so lovely, with the altar adorned and fragrant with flowers, that he asked St. Joseph Cottolengo, "What feast are you celebrating today?" The Saint answered, "We have no feast today; but here in the church it is always a feast day."

St. Francis of Jerome had the task of growing flowers for the Blessed Sacrament altar, and sometimes he made them grow miraculously so that Jesus would not be left without flowers.

"A flower for Jesus" - a beautiful custom! Let us not forgo this gracious gesture of love for Jesus. There may be a small weekly expense, but Jesus will repay it "a hundredfold," and our flowers on the altar will express, by their beauty and fragrance, our presence of love beside Jesus.

As a further point of interest in this regard, St. Augustine tells of a pious custom of his day. After Holy Mass there was a holy competition among the faithful to obtain flowers that had been used on the altar. They would take them home and keep them as relics, because they had been on the altar next to Jesus and were there during His divine sacrifice. Also, St. Jane Frances de Chantal was diligent about always bringing fresh flowers to Jesus; and as soon as those by the tabernacle began to wilt, she took them to her cell to keep at the foot of her crucifix. Ah, what love these practices witnessed!

Let us learn from and imitate the examples of the Saints.

GOD ASKS FOR ADORATION AND REPARATION

When the Angel of Peace appeared to the three children at Fatima, he taught them to make acts of reparation for offences that were being committed against God in the world. He taught them to make acts of adoration of the Holy Trinity and of Jesus in the Blessed Sacrament, in order to make reparation for sins, and to give Glory to God. He taught them the following prayer:

"Most Holy Trinity, Father, Son and Holy Spirit, I adore You profoundly. I offer You the most precious Body, Blood, Soul and Divinity of Our Lord Jesus Christ, present in all the tabernacles of the world, in reparation for all the outrages, sacrileges and indifference by which He is offended. By the infinite merits of His Most Sacred Heart and through the intercession of the Immaculate Heart of Mary, I beg of you the conversion of poor sinners."

Chapter Five
THE ONE WHO GIVES US JESUS

The One Who Gives Us Jesus

Father Gino giving Holy Communion to one of the Sisters of th
new religious order that he founded, assisted by one of the mar
seminarians who have been attracted to San Vittorino by Fathe
Gino.

Who is the one who prepares the Holy Eucharist for us and gives our Lord to us? It is the priest. If there were no priest, there would be no Holy Sacrifice of the Mass, nor Holy Communion, nor the Real Presence of Jesus in the Tabernacle.

And who is the priest? He is the "man of God" (II Tim. 3:17). It is God alone Who chooses him and calls him from among men for a very special vocation. His vocation comes from God, as Aaron's did; nobody can take on himself such a privilege as this" (Heb. 5:4). God puts him apart from everyone else; he is "set apart to preach the Gospel of God" (Rom. 1:1). God distinguishes him with a sacred character that will endure forever, making him "a priest forever" (Heb. 5:6) and bestowing on him the supernatural powers of the ministerial priesthood so that he becomes consecrated exclusively for the things of God. The priest, being "taken from among men, is ordained for men in the things that appertain to God, that he may offer up gifts and sacrifices for sins" (Heb. 5:1).

Poverty, Chastity and Obedience

By his ordination the priest is consecrated in soul and body. He becomes something altogether sacred, likened to the divine priest, Jesus. The priest is thereby a true extension of Jesus, sharing in Jesus' vocation and mission. He fills Jesus' role in the most important works of universal redemption; namely, divine worship and the spread of the Gospel. In his own life he is called to completely reproduce Jesus' life -- the life of One Who was a Virgin, of the One Who was poor, of One Who was crucified. It is by thus making himself like Jesus that he is "the minister of Christ Jesus among the Gentiles" (Rom. 15:16), "a guide and instructor of souls" (Mt. 28:20).

St. Gregory of Nyassa wrote, "One who yesterda was one of the people, becomes their master, the superior, a teacher of sacred things and leader in th sacred mysteries." This happens as a work of th Holy Spirit; for "it is not a man, nor an angel, nor a archangel, nor any created power, but it is the Hol Spirit which bestows the priesthood on a person (St. John Chrysostom). The Holy Spirit makes th priest's soul a likeness of Jesus, empowers the prie to fill the role of Jesus in such wise that "the prie at the altar takes the personal part of Jesus" (S Cyprian), and "has charge of all of God" (St. Joh Chrysostom). Who will be astonished, then, if th priestly dignity is declared "heavenly" (Cassian "divine" (St. Dionysius), "infinite" (St. Ephrem something "lovingly venerated by the angels" (S Gregory Nazianzen), so great that "when the prie conducts the Divine Sacrifice, angels station then selves about him and in a choir they chant a hymn (praise in honor of the Victim Who is sacrificed (St. John Chrysostom). And this happens at ever Mass!

Respect and Veneration

We know that St. Francis of Assisi was unwillin to become a priest because he considered himse unworthy of such a lofty vocation. He honore priests with a special devotion, considering them h "lords", "because in them he saw only "the Son God." His love for the Eucharist merged with his lo for the priest who consecrates and administers t Body and Blood of Jesus. He paid special veneratic to the priest's hands, which he used to always ki on his knees very devoutly. He used to even kiss priest's feet and even the footprints where one ha walked.

The veneration of the priest's consecrated hands, reverently kissed by the faithful, has always existed in the Church. It is noteworthy that during the persecution of the first centuries, one particular outrage to bishops and priests consisted in cutting off their hands so that they could no longer perform the consecration nor give blessings. Christians used to go find those amputated hands and keep them as relics with preservative spices. Kissing the priest's hands is a delicate expression of faith and love for Jesus whom the priest represents. The more faith and love there is among the people, the more they will venture to kneel before the priest and kiss those "holy and venerable hands" (the Roman Canon), in which Jesus lovingly makes Himself present every day.

"Oh the venerable dignity of the priest," exclaims St. Augustine, "in whose hands the Son of God becomes incarnate as He did in the Virgin's womb!" The holy Curé of Ars said, "We attach great value to objects that are handed down and kept at Loretto, as the holy Virgin's porridge bowl and that of the Child Jesus. But the priest's fingers, which have touched the adorable Body of Jesus Christ, which have been put into the chalice where His Blood was and into the ciborium where His body was -- might not these fingers be more precious?" Perhaps we never thought of it before. But it is really so. Examples of the Saints confirm this answer.

In an ecstasy the Ven. Catherine Vannini saw angels gather about the priest's hands during Mass and support them at the elevation of the Host and the chalice. We can imagine the reverence and affection with which this Venerable Servant of God used to kiss those hands!

The Queen, St. Hedwig, every morning attended all the Holy Masses that were celebrated in the Chapel the court, displaying gratitude and reverence toward the priests who had celebrated Holy Mass. She used to offer them hospitality, kiss their hands devotedly, see that they were fed, and show them every honor. She would show deep feeling when exclaiming, "God bless the one who made Jesus come down from Heaven and gave Him to me!"

St. Paschal Baylon was porter in a Monastery. Each time a priest arrived, the holy lay brother knelt and reverently kissed both his hands. People said of him - as they did of St. Francis -- that he had devotion for the consecrated hands of priests. He judged that those hands had power to ward off evils and draw down blessings for the one who would treat them with veneration, since they are hands that Jesus makes use of.

And was it not an edifying sight to see how Padre Pio of Pietrelcina wanted to affectionately kiss priest's hands, even suddenly seizing them unexpectedly? We are impressed, too, by the example of another Servant of God, the priest Don Dolindo Ruotolo, who would not admit that any priest could refuse "the charity" of letting someone kiss his hands.

We know that God has often rewarded this act of veneration by means of true miracles. We read in the life of St. Ambrose, that one day after he had celebrated Holy Mass the Saint was approached by a woman afflicted with paralysis who wanted to kiss his hands. The woman had great confidence in those hands that had consecrated the Eucharist; and she was cured at once. Likewise at Benevento a woman who had suffered paralysis for fifteen years asked Pope Leo IX to let her drink the water he had used during Holy Mass to wash his fingers. The holy Pontiff granted the request, which was made quite humbly, like that of the woman of Canaan who sked Jesus for "the crumbs that fall from the table of their masters" (Mt. 15:27). And she, too, was nstantly healed.

The faith of the Saints was something that was ruly great and produced results. They lived by aith (Rom. 1:17) and conducted themselves by a aith and a love that allowed no holding back when hey dealt with Jesus. For them the priest represen-ed nothing more nor less than Jesus. "In priests I ee the Son of God," said St. Francis of Assisi. The oly Curé of Ars remarked in a sermon, "Every ime I see a priest, I think of Jesus." When she vould speak of a priest, St. Mary Magdalen di Pazzi sed to refer to him as "this Jesus". Because of this steem St. Catherine of Siena used to kiss the floor r ground where a priest had passed. One day St. 'eronica Giuliani saw the priest mount the stair-vay of the monastery to take Holy Communion to he sick, and she knelt at the foot of the stairs, and nen climbed the steps on her knees, kissing each tep and moistening it with tears that her love pro-uced. What examples of love!

The holy Cure of Ars used to say, "If I met a priest nd an angel, I would pay respect to the priest first, nd then to the angel... If it were not for the priest, he Passion and Death of Jesus would not help us... 'hat good would a chest full of gold be if there were o one to open it? The priest has the key to the hea-enly treasures..." Who causes Jesus to come down in he white Hosts? Who puts Jesus into our taber-acles? Who gives Jesus to our souls? Who purifies ur hearts so that we can receive Jesus? It is the iest, only the priest. He is the one "who serves the bernacle" (Heb. 13:10), who has the "ministry of conciliation" (II Cor. 5:18), "who is for you a inister of Jesus Christ" (Col. 1:7) and dispenser "of the mysteries of God" (I Cor. 4:1). Oh, how many instances could be reported of heroic priest sacrificing themselves in order to give Jesus to their flock! We report here one case out of many.

Some years ago in a parish in Brittany, an old pastor was lying on his deathbed. Also at that time one of his parishioners was nearing the end of his life, who was among those that had strayed from God and the Church. The pastor was distressed because he could not get up and go to him; so he sent the assistant pastor to him, admonishing him to remind the dying man that once he had promised that he would not die without the Sacraments. The parishioner, hearing this, excused himself with the words, "I promised that to the pastor, not to you." The assistant pastor had to leave the dying man and reported his answer to the pastor. The pastor was not daunted, though he realized he himself had only a few hours left, he arranged to be carried to the home of the sinner. He was brought into the house succeeded in hearing the dying man's confession and gave him Our Lord in Holy Communion. Then he said to him, "Farewell till we meet in Paradise!" The courageous pastor was carried back to his rectory on a stretcher. When he arrived, the covers over him were raised, but the priest did not move. He had died.

Let us hold the priest in veneration and be grateful to him because he brings us Our Lord. Above all let us pray for the fulfillment of his lofty mission, which is the mission of Jesus; "As the Father hath sent me, I also send you" (John 20:21). It is a divine mission which overwhelms the mind when one thinks deeply on the love which inspired it. The priest is "likened unto the Son of God" (Heb. 7:3), and the holy Cure of Ars used to say that "only in Heaven will we measure the full great ness of this. If we appreciated it here on earth we would die, not of fright but of love ... After God, the priest is all."

But this sublime grandeur brings an enormous responsibility which weighs down on the impoverished human nature of the priest, a human nature fully identical with that of every other man. "The priest," said St. Bernard, "by nature is like all other men; by dignity he surpasses every other man on earth; by his conduct he ought to compare with the angels."

A divine calling, a sublime mission, an angelic life, lofty rank -- what immense weights, all on poor moral shoulders! "The priesthood is a cross and a martyrdom" was a good description given by that excellent priest and Servant of God, Don Edward Poppe.

Consider what a weight of responsibility for the salvation of souls is laid upon the priest. His task is to bring the faith to unbelievers, to convert sinners, to give fervor to the lukewarm, to stimulate the good to become ever better, to make holy people walk on the highest levels. Now how can he do all this unless he maintains a true union, an identity, with Jesus? This is why Padre Pio of Pietrelcina used to say, "The priest is either a saint or a devil." He either moves souls to holiness or to ruin. What incalculable ruin does the priest not bring who profanes his vocation by unworthy conduct or who ventures to trample on it by renouncing his status as one consecrated and chosen by the Lord (John 15:16)!

In the canonical proceedings for the canonization of St. John Vianney, it is written that the holy Curé shed many tears "as he thought of the ruin of priests who do not correspond to the holiness of their vocation." Padre Pio of Pietrelcina described heart-rending

visions of the frightful pains Jesus suffered for th
guilt of unworthy and unfaithful priests.

We know that St. Therese of Lisieux, the angeli
Carmelite nun, just before she died made her las
Holy Communion for this sublime intention -- t
obtain the return of a stray priest who had renounce
his vocation. And we know that this priest died re
pentant, invoking Jesus.

We know that souls are not rare, especially virgina
souls, who have offered themselves as victims to b
sacrificed to God for priests. These souls are favore
by Jesus in an altogether singular way. But let us
too, offer prayers and sacrifices for priests, for thos
in danger and for those who stand more firm and se
cure, for those who are straying and for those wh
are advancing in perfection.

And in particular, every time we see a priest at th
altar, let us also pray to the Madonna, in the word
of the Venerable Charles Giacinto, "O dear Madonna
lend your heart to that priest so that he can worthil
celebrate the Mass." Better yet, rather let us pra
that every priest is able to imitate St. Gaetano, wh
used to prepare himself for the celebration of Hol
Mass by uniting himself so closely to Mary Mo
Holy, that it was said of him, "He celebrates Ma
as if he were Her." And, indeed, as the Madonn
welcomed Jesus into Her arms at Bethlehem, sim
larly the priest receives Jesus in his hands in th
Holy Mass. As the Madonna offered Jesus the Victi
on Calvary, similarly the priest offers the Divi
Lamb that is sacrificed on the altar. As the Madonn
gave Jesus to mankind, similarly the priest gives
Jesus in Holy Communion. Thus St. Bonaventu
rightly declares that every priest at the altar ought
be identified with the Madonna; for, since it w
by Her means that this Most Holy Body has been

en to us, so by the priest's hands It must be offered."
And St. Francis of Assisi said that for all priests the
Madonna represents the mirror of their sanctity,
given the close proximity there is between the Incarnation of the Word in Mary's womb, and the
consecration of the Eucharist in the priest's hands.

...Mary, of whom was born Jesus" (Mt. 1:16)

Chapter Six

THE BREAD THAT OUR HEAVENLY
MOTHER GIVES US

The Holy Eucharist is the Bread that comes from our Heavenly Mother. It is Bread produced by Mary from the flour of Her immaculate flesh, kneaded into dough with her virginal milk. St. Augustine wrote "Jesus took His Flesh from the flesh of Mary.

We know, too, that united to the Divinity in the Eucharist there is Jesus' Body and Blood taken from the body and blood of the Blessed Virgin. Therefore at every Holy Communion we receive, it would be quite correct, and a very beautiful thing, to take notice of our Holy Mother's sweet and mysterious presence, inseparably united with Jesus in the Host. Jesus is always the Son She adores. He is Flesh

Her flesh and Blood of Her blood. If Adam could call Eve when she had been taken from his rib, "bone of my bone and flesh of my flesh" (Gen. 2:23), cannot the holy Virgin Mary even more rightly call Jesus 'Flesh of my flesh and Blood of my blood"?

Taken from the "intact Virgin" as says St. Thomas Aquinas, the flesh of Jesus is the maternal flesh of Mary, the blood of Jesus is the maternal blood of Mary. Therefore it will never be possible to separate Jesus from Mary.

For this reason at every Holy Mass which is celebrated, the Blessed Virgin can repeat with truth to Jesus in the Host and in the Chalice, "You are my Son today I have generated you" (Ps 2:7). And justly St. Augustine teaches us that in the Eucharist "Mary extends and perpetuates Her Divine Maternity", while St. Albert the Great exhorts with love, "My soul if you wish to experience intimacy with Mary let yourself be carried between Her arms and nourished with Her blood" ... Go with this ineffable haste thought to the banquet of God and you will find in the Blood of the Son the nourishment of the Mother.

Many Saints and theologians (St. Pater Damien, St. Bernard, St. Bonaventure, St. Bernadine ...) say that Jesus instituted the Eucharist above all for Mary and then through Mary, the Universal Mediatrix of All Graces, for all of us. And from Mary therefore Jesus comes to be given to us day by day; and in Jesus is always the Immaculate flesh and the Virginal Blood of His Most Holy Mother which penetrates into our hearts and inebriates our souls. In an ecstacy during the celebration of Holy Mass, St. Ignatius of Loyola contemplated one day the reality revealed by this most sweet truth and he remained celestially moved for a long time.

Furthermore, if we reflect that Jesus, the Fruit of Mary's immaculate womb, constitutes all of Mary's love, all of Her sweetness, all of Her tenderness, Her whole riches, Her whole life, then we see that when we receive Him we cannot fail to also receive Her who, by ties of the highest love, as well as by ties of flesh and blood, forms with Jesus one unity, one whole, as She is always and inseparably "leaning upon Her Beloved" (cant. 8:5). Is it not true that love, and above all divine love, unites and unifies? And aside from the Unity in the bosom of the Blessed Trinity, can we think of a unity more close and total than that between Jesus and the Virgin Mary?

Mary's purity, Her virginity, Her tender ways, Her sweet manner, Her love, and even the very features of Her heavenly face -- all these we find in Jesus; for the most holy humanity assumed by the Word is wholly and only Mary's humanity, on account of the great mystery of the virginal Conception accomplished by the Holy Spirit, Who made Mary Jesus' Mother, while consecrating Her as a Virgin that would be forever undefiled and glorious in soul and body.

And thus "The Eucharist," writes St. Albert the Great, "produces impulses of a love that is angelic and It has the unique power to put in souls a holy feeling of tenderness toward the Queen of Angels. She has given us what is Flesh of Her flesh and Bone of Her bone, and in the Eucharist She continues to give us this sweet, virginal, heavenly banquet.

Finally, in the eternal generation of the Word in the bosom of the Trinity, the Father gives Himself wholly to the Son, Who is "Mirror of the Father", similarly in the temporal generation of the same Word in the bosom of humanity, the Mother of God gives Herself wholly to the Son, to Her Jesus, "the virginal Flower of the Virgin Mother" (Pius XII). And the Son in His turn gives Himself wholly to the Mother, making Himself similar to Her and making Her "fully Godlike" (St. Peter Damian).

St. Peter Julian Eymard, that Saint so totally devoted to the Eucharist, declared that even in this world, after Jesus' Ascension into Heaven, the Blessed Virgin "lived a life in and by the Blessed Sacrament;" and thus he liked to call Her "Our Lady of the Blessed Sacrament." And Padre Pio of Pietrelcina would sometimes say to his spiritual children, "Do you not see the Madonna always beside the tabernacle?" And how could She fail to be there — She who "stood by the cross of Jesus" on Calvary (John 19:25)? Therefore St. Alphonsus Liguori, in his book of devotions, used to always join a visit to the Blessed Virgin Mary to each visit to Jesus in the Holy Eucharist. And Saint Maximilian M. Kolbe used to recommend that when we go before Jesus in the Blessed Sacrament, we never fail to remember Mary's presence, calling on Her and associating ourselves with Her, at least seeing to it that Her sweet name comes to mind.

In the life of the Dominican friar, St. Hyacinth, we read that once in order to avoid a profanation of the Blessed Sacrament, the Saint hastened to the tabernacle to take out the ciborium containing the sacred particles, in order to put it in a safer place. When, hugging Jesus in the Eucharist close to his breast, he was about to leave the altar, he heard a voice coming from the statue of the Blessed Virgin which was next to the altar, saying, "What? Would you take Jesus away without taking me?" The Saint halted in surprise. He understood the message, but he did not know how he could manage to carry Mary's statue too. Puzzled, he drew near the statue to see if he could take it with his one free hand. There was no need to strain himself, for the statue became as light as a feather. There is a precious lesson in this miracle: When we take Mary along with Jesus, she adds absolutely no weight or cost, for in a wonderful way they abide in one another (John 6:57).

The reply St. Bernadette Soubirous gave was very beautiful, when someone put this tricky question to her: "What would please you more, to receive Holy Communion, or to see the Madonna in the grotto?" The little Saint thought for a minute and then answered, "What a strange question! The two cannot be separated. Jesus and Mary always go together."

The Madonna and the Holy Eucharist are by the nature of things united inseparably "even to the end of the world" (Mt. 28:20). For Mary with Her body and soul is the heavenly "tabernacle of God" (Apoc. 21:3). She is the incorruptible Host, "holy and immaculate" (Eph. 5:27), who, with Her very self clothes the Word of God made Man. St. Germain ventured to call Her "sweet paradise of God." According to a pious opinion, supported by the ecstasies and visions of St. Veronica Giuliani and especially those of Blessed Magdalen Martinengo, within Her breast the Blessed Virgin in paradise preserves and will always preserve Jesus in a visible Host; and this is for Her "eternal consolation, is an occasion of rejoicing for all the blessed inhabitants of Heaven, and in particular is an everlasting joy to all devotees of the Blessed Sacrament." This is represented in the "Madonna Mediatrice Universale," which Mothe

Speranza in recent times has painted and which has been placed in the Shrine at Collevalenza. It is the same as the image often reproduced in monstrances (sacred stands for exposing the Holy Eucharist for adoration) of the last century, which represent the Madonna, and make a place in her breast for the visible cavity in which the consecrated Host is put. "Blessed is the womb that bore Thee!" cried the woman amid the crowd (Lk. 11:27). Thus in some of the churches in France the tabernacle used to be encased in a statue of Our Lady of the Assumption. The significance is quite clear: it is always the Blessed Virgin Mary who gives us Jesus, Who is the blessed Fruit of Her virginal womb and the Heart of Her Immaculate Heart. And She will forever continue to carry Jesus in the Holy Eucharist within Her breast so as to present Him for the joyful contemplation of the Saints in Heaven, to whom it is even now given to see His divine Person in the Eucharistic Species, according to the teaching of the Angelic Doctor, St. Thomas Aquinas.

It is in the Eucharist, and especially in Holy Communion, that our union with the Madonna becomes a full and loving conformity with Her. We receive Her devoted care and protection along with the Blessed Sacrament. Her tender attentions overlook nothing as Christ is united to each of us, Her children, moving Her to pour out all Her motherly love on our souls and bodies. The great St. Hilary, Father and Doctor of the Church, wrote this excellent passage: "The greatest joy that we can give Mary is that of bearing Jesus in the Blessed Sacrament within our breast." Her motherly union with Jesus becomes a union also with whoever is united to Jesus, especially in Holy Communion. And what can give as much joy to one who loves, as union with the person loved? And we — do we not happen to be beloved children of the heavenly Mother?

When we go before Jesus on the altar, we always find Him "with Mary His Mother," as the Magi did at Bethlehem (Mt. 2:11). And Jesus in the sacred Host, from the altar of our hearts, can repeat to each of us what He said to St. John the Evangelist from the altar of Calvary, "Behold thy Mother" (John 19:27).

St. Augustine beautifully illustrates even better how Mary makes Herself our own and unites Herself to each one of us in Holy Communion. He says, "The Word is the Food of the angels. Men have not the strength to feed It to themselves, nor need they do so. What is needed is a mother who may eat this supersubstantial Bread, transform it into her milk, and in this way feed her poor children. This mother is Mary. She nourishes herself with the Word and transforms It into the Sacred Humanity. She transforms It into Flesh and Blood, i.e., into this sweetest of milk which is called the Eucharist."

Thus it is quite natural that the great as well as the lesser Marian shrines always foster devotion to the Holy Eucharist, so much so that they can also be called Eucharistic shrines. Lourdes, Fatima, Loretto, Pompei, come to mind, where crowds approach the altar in almost endless lines to receive Mary's blessed Fruit. It cannot be otherwise; for there is no bond so close and so sweet with the Madonna, as the one realized in receiving the Holy Eucharist. Jesus and Mary "always go together," as St. Bernadette said.

Remember, too, that at Fatima the Madonna asked that, together with the holy Rosary, there be above all the Communion of Reparation for all the offences and outrages which Her Immaculate Heart receives. She is looking for loving hearts that want to console Her by welcoming Her into their home, as St. John

...he Evangelist did (John 19:27). We truly welcome ...er in the home of our hearts with the warmest hospitality, the hospitality dearest to Her, every time we invite Her company by way of our receiving Jesus in Holy Communion, when we present Her with the ...ving, true Jesus for Her great comfort and delight. We need to appreciate what a great grace this is to ...ave the Madonna's full care and attention with Jesus ...nd in Jesus. Ah, St. Ambrose wanted all Christians ...o have "Mary's soul to magnify the Lord and Mary's ...pirit to exult in God"! This is the favor granted us in ...he noblest way in every Holy Communion. Let us ...eflect on it with love and gratitude.

One of the old monstrances made in the figure of ...Mary carrying the Holy Eucharist in Her breast has ...hese words inscribed on its base: "O Christian who ...omest full of faith to receive the Bread of life, eat It ...orthily, and remember that It was fashioned out of ...Mary's pure blood." Mary can quite rightfully beckon ...o us and speak to us in the words of the inspired ...rophet, "Come and eat my bread, drink the wine I ...ave prepared" (Prov. 9:5). Saint Maximilian M. ...olbe wanted to convey the thought of this passage ...hen he proposed that all altars of the Blessed ...acrament be surmounted with a statue of the Im- ...aculate Virgin with her arms extended to invite us ...l to come eat the Bread that She herself had made.

With beautiful imagery, St. Gregory of Tours said ...at Mary's Immaculate bosom is the heavenly cup- ...oard, well-stocked with the Bread of Life that was ...ade in order to feed Her children. "Blessed is the ...omb that bore Thee and the paps that gave Thee ...ck!" exclaimed a certain woman to Jesus (Lk. ...1:27). The Immaculate Virgin carried Jesus within ...er while His Body was being formed from Her own ...esh and Her own blood. Thus every time we go to ...oly Communion, something sweet to recall is that

113

Jesus in the Blessed Sacrament is the Bread of Life produced from Mary with the flour of Her Immaculate flesh, kneaded with the admixture of Her virginal milk. She has made this for us, Her children. And we realize more fully our brotherhood with one another as we all partake of this savory, exquisite Bread of our Mother.

Chapter Seven
PRAYERS BEFORE THE BLESSED SACRAMENT

Holy Communion: Preparation; Thanksgiving

Holy Communion with Mary

Before the Holy Eucharist:
The Visit to the Blessed Sacrament
Spiritual Communion
Visit to the Blessed Virgin Mary

Holy Communion

Preparation

Faith

My Lord Jesus Christ, with all my soul I believe that You are really present in the Sacrament of the Altar. I believe it because You have said it - You Whom I adore as Supreme Truth. Addressing You in the sacred Host, I declare with St. Peter: Thou art the Christ, the Son of the living God.

Adoration

I adore You and acknowledge You as my Creator, Lord, Redeemer, and my Supreme and only Good.

Hope

O Lord, I hope that as You have given Yourself wholly to me in this divine Sacrament, You will exercise Your mercy and grant me the graces I need in order to gain Paradise more easily.

Love

O Lord, I love You with all my heart above all things because You are my infinitely lovable God. Forgive me for having loved You so little up to now. I would like to love You with the ardor of the Seraphim and with the Heart of Mary Immaculate, Your Mother and mine.

For Your sake, O Jesus, I wish to love my neighbour as myself.

Humility

O Lord, I am not worthy to receive You, but only say the word, and my soul will be healed.

Sorrow

Before approaching You, O Jesus, I ask You once more for the pardon of my sins. You have loved me so much as to die for me, and I have been so evil, and have offended You countless times. Have mercy on me! Forgive me! By Your grace wipe away every smallest stain of sin. I wish to approach You with an angelic purity so that I can worthily receive Thee.

Desire

My God, come into my soul that You may make it holy. My God, come into my heart to purify it. My God, enter my body in order to keep it and so that I will never separate myself from Your love.

Destroy everything You see in me that is unworthy of Your presence and can hinder Your grace and Your love.

(Remember within a few minutes Jesus will be within you. This is the most beautiful and greatest moment of your day.

Be well prepared. Present to Jesus a heart ardent in his love and desire for Him. Be fully aware that you are undeserving of such great favor, and do not go to communion with your soul stained with mortal sin.

Endeavor to let your Holy Communion be during Holy Mass. But if this is not possible, go ahead and receive Holy Communion outside Mass, so that you will not miss a day without receiving Jesus.

Remember that a fervent Holy Communion 1) preserves and increases sanctifying grace in you, 2) takes away venial sins, 3) protects you from falling into mortal sin, 4) brings you consolation and comfort, with an increase of charity and hope of eternal life.

Thanksgiving

(As Jesus is now with you, you have become a living tabernacle. Keep recollected and adore your Lord. Express to Him the fullness of your joy in possessing Him. Open your heart to Him and speak to Him with great confidence.)

Prayer

O Jesus, I find myself deeply moved in the presence of Your infinite love. How grateful I am to You! I do not know how to do anything else but repeat: Thank You, O Jesus! What shall I do for You O Lord, in return for Your Gift?

I hear Your sweet voice repeating to me: "My son give Me thy heart" (Prov. 23:26). Yes, Lord, I offer You my heart and my soul. I consecrate to You my whole life. I want to belong entirely to You forever.

To Jesus Crucified

Behold, O good and most sweet Jesus, I cast myself upon my knees in Thy sight and with the most fervent desire of my soul, I pray and beseech Thee that Thou wouldst impress upon my heart lively sentiments of Faith, Hope, and Charity, with true contrition for my sins and a firm purpose of amendment; while with deep affection and grief of soul I ponder within myself and mentally contemplate Thy five most precious wounds, having before my eyes that which David the Prophet spoke of Thee, my good Jesus: "They have pierced My hands and My feet, they have numbered all My bones." (Our Father, Hail Mary)

Soul of Christ, make me holy. Body of Christ, save me. Blood of Christ, inebriate me. Water from the side of Christ, cleanse me. Passion of Christ, strengthen me. O good Jesus, hear me. Within Thy wounds, shelter me. Do not permit me to be separated from Thee. From the wicked enemy defend me. At the hour of my death, call me, and bid me to come to Thee, that with Thy Saints I may praise Thee forever. Amen.

Prayer of Saint Bonaventure

Pierce, O most sweet Lord Jesus Christ, mine inmost soul with the most joyous and healthful wound of Thy love, with true, serene, and most holy apostolic charity, that my soul may ever languish and melt with love and longing for Thee, that it may yearn for Thee and faint for Thy courts, and long to be dissolved and to be with Thee. Grant that my soul may hunger after Thee, the bread of angels, the refreshment of holy souls, our daily and supersubstantial bread, having all sweetness and savour and every delight of taste. Let my heart ever hunger after and feed upon Thee, whom the angels desire to look upon, and may my inmost soul be filled with the sweetness of Thy savour. May it ever thirst after Thee, the fountain of life, the fountain of wisdom and knowledge, the fountain of eternal light, the torrent of pleasure, the richness of the house of God. May it ever compass Thee, seek Thee, find Thee, run to Thee, attain to Thee, meditate upon Thee, speak of Thee, and do all things to the praise and glory of Thy Holy name, with humility and discretion, with love and delight, with readiness and affection, and with perseverance unto the end. Be Thou alone ever my hope and my whole confidence, my riches, my delight, my pleasure and my joy; my rest and tranquility; my peace, my sweetness and my fragrance; my sweet savour, my food and refreshment; my refuge and my help; my wisdom, my portion, my possession and my treasure, in whom may my mind and my heart be ever fixed and firm, and rooted immovably. Amen.

Prayer of St. Thomas Aquinas

I give Thee thanks O holy Lord, Almighty Father, Eternal God, who has vouschafed, not through any merits of mine, but out of the condescension of Thy great mercy, to nourish me a sinner, thine unworthy servant, with the precious Body and Blood of thy Son our Lord Jesus Christ. I pray that this Holy Communion be not to me a condemnation unto punishment, but a saving plea unto forgiveness. May It be unto me the armour of faith and the shield of good purpose. May It cause the emptying out of my vices and the extinction of all concupiscence and lust; an increase of charity and patience, of humility and obedience, and of all virtues. May It be unto me a strong defence against the snares of all my enemies, visible and invisible; the perfect quieting of all my evil impulses both fleshly and spiritual; may It cause me to firmly cleave unto Thee the one true God; and may It make my death holy and happy. And I pray Thee that Thou wouldst vouschafe to bring me, a sinner, to that ineffable banquet, where Thou, with Thy Son and Thy Holy Spirit, art to Thy saints true light, fulness of content, eternal joy, gladness without alloy, and perfect happiness. I ask this through the same Christ our Lord. Amen.

HOLY COMMUNION WITH MARY

(Meditating on the Hail Mary)

Preparation

O holy Virgin, I am about to receive your Jesus. I wish my heart were like yours when you became Mother of the Savior at the time of the Annunciation of the Angel.

Hail Mary

I greet you, good Mother. Allow me to unite myself with you to adore Jesus. Lend me your affections, your sentiments. Moreover I ask you, in fact, to adore Him for me. Hail, O true Body of Jesus, born of the Virgin Mary! I believe, and I adore You.

Full of grace

You, Mary, were worthy to receive the all-holy God, for you were full of grace from the first moment of your life. But I am poor and sinful. My evil ways make me unfit to go to Communion. O my Mother, cover me with your merits and lead me to Jesus.

The Lord is with Thee

The Lord is with thee, O most Holy Virgin. By your ardent longing you drew Him down from Heaven into your heart. Instill also in my heart an ardent longing and an insatiable hunger for Jesus, so that I can truly say, "Come, O my Jesus, I long for You with the heart of Mary, Your Mother and mine."

Blessed art thou among women

Blessed art thou, O Mary, who have never known the remorse that comes from committing sin; for you are free of every kind of sin and imperfection. But I know I have sinned, and I am not sure that I have been sufficiently sorry. Make me understand the evil of my sins and the goodness of God whom I have offended. I weep for my sins. Present me thus penitent to your Jesus.

And blessed is the Fruit of thy womb

Ah, good Mother! What a great gift you have given us in giving us our Savior, Jesus! And behold, He wants to come to me to make me an especially beloved child of your heart. I go with confidence to receive Him, and I say to Him: "My Jesus, I abandon myself to You. Come to give me strength to serve You faithfully, and the hope of enjoying You forever with Your Mother in Heaven."

Jesus

Grant, oh Mother, that I experience those sentiments that you experienced as you lived in Jesus' company, as you called Him by name. I am now about to receive Him. Allow me to be able to say to Him: "Come, O my Jesus. You will find in me the same welcome that You had from Your Mother on earth. I hope that through Her intercession You will welcome me into Heaven."

Thanksgiving

Holy Mary, Mother of God

O my Mother, how happy I am to be united with my Jesus! But how do I deserve to have my Lord come down to me? O Mary, who are holy and Immaculate, offer Him worthy thanks for me.

O thou who, from the first perceived the heart beats of that Jesus Whom I now welcome within me thou who loved Him more than all the Saints together have loved Him, and who lived for Him alone when you were on earth, grant that I may now share your sentiments and your love.

And Thou, O Jesus, accept the love of Your Mother as though it were my own and do not deny me a tender glance while I also say to Thee with all my heart, "I love Thee."

Pray for us sinners

Pray for me, O Mary. At this time unite your prayers to mine. And now that Jesus has come into my heart, ready to grant me all graces, I wish to ask Him above all that I never separate myself from Him by sin. And you, O Mary, preserve me from evil, and be my refuge in temptation.

Now

For now and from now on, beloved Mother, I beg for all the graces that are profitable to my soul. Obtain for me this favor: that I be clothed with the virtues of goodness and meekness and that my life be one of spotless purity.

And at the hour of our death

From now on my prayer, O Jesus, is that I may receive You worthily at the time of my death and that my death may be a holy one. I accept it, when and how You shall send it to me — I welcome it in union with Your sacrifice fulfilled on the Cross. I accept it in order to submit myself to the divine Will, for the glory of God, for my salvation, and for the salvation of souls.

O Sorrowful Virgin, assist me as you have assisted Jesus in His last agony.

"Amen"

"So be it." O Jesus, here is the word that I want to repeat at every instant, both during my youth and throughout my life. May Thy Will be done always. And all that You provide is the best thing for me, and from now on I accept it and give You thanks. Amen.

BEFORE THE HOLY EUCHARIST

The Visit to the Blessed Sacrament

My Lord Jesus Christ, Who, for the love You bear towards men, remain in this Sacrament night and day, filled with compassion and love, waiting, calling, and welcoming all who come to visit Thee: I believe that Thou art present in the Sacrament of the Altar; I adore Thee from the abyss of my nothingness, and I thank Thee for all the graces Thou hast given me, particularly for having given me Thyself in this Sacrament, for having given me Thy Most Holy Mother Mary as my Advocate, and for having called me to visit Thee in this church.

I pay reverence to Thy most loving Heart today, and this for three purposes: **first**, in thanksgiving for this great Gift; **second**, to make reparation for all the outrages Thou hast received from all Thy enemies in this Sacrament; **third**, I intend by this visit to adore Thee in all the places on earth in which Thou art present in this Sacrament, and in which Thou art least honored and most abandoned.

My Jesus, I love Thee with all my heart. I repent of having so often displeased Thy infinite Goodness in the past. I resolve with the help of Thy grace not to offend Thee ever again in the future; and for the present, poor sinner though I be, I consecrate myself wholly to Thee. I renounce and surrender to Thee my whole will, my affections, my desires, and all that belongs to me. From this day forward do whatever You please with me and what belongs to me. I ask and wish only of Thee Thy holy love, final perseverance and the perfect fulfillment of Thy Will.

I recommend to Thee the souls in Purgatory especially those most devoted to the Most Blessed Sacrament and to the Blessed Virgin Mary. I also recommend to Thee all poor sinners.

O my beloved Savior, I unite all my affections with the affections of Thy most loving Heart, and thus united, I offer them to Thy Eternal Father, and I beg Him in Thy name that for love of Thee He accept them and heed them. Amen.

Spiritual Communion

My Jesus, I believe that You are really present in the Most Blessed Sacrament. I love Thee above all things, and I desire to possess Thee within my soul. Since I cannot now receive Thee sacramentally, come at least spiritually into my heart.

(Make a brief pause, and during it unite yourself with Jesus.)

I embrace Thee as being already there and unite myself wholly to Thee. Never, never permit me to be separated from Thee. Amen.

Visit to the Blessed Virgin Mary

O most holy, Immaculate Virgin and my Mother Mary, to Thee who are the Mother of my Lord, the Queen of the world, the Advocate, the hope, the refuge of sinners, I, who am the most miserable of all sinners, have recourse today. I venerate Thee, O great Queen, and I thank Thee for all the graces Thou hast conferred on me until now, especially for having delivered me from hell, which I have so often deserved. I love Thee, O Most amiable Lady, and because of the love I bear Thee, I promise to serve Thee always and do all in my power to make Thee loved by others. I place in Thee all my hopes; I confide my salvation to Thy care. Accept me as Thy servant, and shelter me under Thy mantle, O Mother of Mercy. And since You are so powerful with God, deliver me from all temptations, or obtain for me the strength to triumph over them until my death.

Of Thee I ask a perfect love of Jesus Christ. From Thee I hope to die a good death. O Mary, my Mother, for the love You bear to God, I beg You to help me always, but especially at the last moment of my life. Leave me not, I beseech Thee, until Thou seest me safe in Heaven, blessing Thee and singing Thy mercies for all eternity. Amen. So I hope. So may it be.

--St. Alphonsus Liguori

SUPPLEMENT

The Eucharistic Miracle of Lanciano

Ancient Anxanum, the city of the Frentanese, has contained for over twelve centuries the first and greatest Eucharistic Miracle of the Catholic Church. This wondrous event took place in the 8th century A.D. in the little Church of St. Legontian, as a divine response to a Basilian monk's doubt about Jesus' Real Presence in the Eucharist.

During Holy Mass, after the two-fold consecration, the host was changed into live Flesh and the wine was changed into live Blood, which coagulated into five globules, irregular and differing in shape and size.

The Host-Flesh, as can be very distinctly observed today, has the same dimensions as the large host used today in the Latin church; it is light brown and appears rose-colored when lighted from the back. The Blood is coagulated and has an earthy color resembling the yellow of ochre. Since 1713 the Flesh has been reserved in an artistic silver ostensorium delicately embossed by an artisan of the Neapolitan school.

The Blood is enclosed in a rich and very old cup made of Rock-crystal.

The Friars Minor Conventual have been the custodians of the Sanctuary since 1252; their appointment was the wish of Bishop Landulf of Chieti; their appointment was confirmed by a Pontifical Bull dated April, 20. 1252,

The church was in charge of the Basilian monks until 1176; from 1176 until 1252 the Benedictines staffed the church.

In 1258 the Franciscans built the present church. In 1700 its architectural style was changed from romanesque-gothic to baroque.

The "Miracle" was first reserved in a chapel situated at the side of the main altar.

Then, from 1636 it was reserved in a side-altar of the nave which still contains the old iron chest and the commemorative inscription.

In 1902 it was transferred into the present monumental marble altar which the people of Lanciano had erected.

Various ecclesiastical investigations ("Recognitions") were conducted since 1574.

In 1970 there took place a scientific investigation by the most illustrious scientist, prof. Odoardo Linoli, Eminent Professor in Anatomy and Pathological Histology and in Chemistry and Clinical Microscopy.

He was assisted by Prof. Ruggero Bertelli of the University of Siena.

The analyses were conducted with absolute and unquestionable scientific precision and they were documented with a series of microscopic photographs which were rendered a matter of public domain by the esteemed Prof. Linoli himself in a conference held on March 4, 1971 in the church of the Miracle.

These analyses sustained the following conclusions:

— **The Flesh is real Flesh. The Blood is real Blood.**
— **The Flesh consist of the muscular tissue of the the heart (myocardium).**
— **The Flesh and the Blood belong to the human species.**
— **The Flesh and the Blood have the same blood-type (AB).**
— **In the Blood there were found proteins in the same normal proportions (percentage-wise) as are found in the sero-proteic make-up of fresh normal blood.**
— **In the Blood there were also found these minerals: chlorides, phosphorus, magnesium, potassium, sodium and calcium.**
— **The preservation of the Flesh and of the Blood, which were left in their natural state for twelve centuries (= i.e. without any chemical preservatives) and exposed to the action of atmospheric and biological agents, remains and extraordinary phenomenon.**

In conclusion, it may be said that Science, when called upon to testify, has given a certain and thorough response as regards the authenticity of the Eucharistic Miracle of Lanciano.

Imprimatur: †Leopoldo Teofili
   Archbishop of Lanciano.

For information, books, pamphlets, slides, postcards, souvenirs of the Sanctuary, please apply to:

SANTUARIO DEL MIRACOLO EUCARISTICO
FRATI MINORI CONVENTUALI
66034 LANCIANO (Ch) Italy

128   A full length book in English about this Eucharistic miracle is available from the publisher of this book.

Title	1 copy	5 copies	10 copies	25 copies	50 copies	100 copies
The Glories of Mary	$4.00 each	$3.00 each	$2.50 each	$2.00 each	$1.75 each	$1.25 each
The Way of Divine Love	$4.00 each	$2.50 each	$2.00 each	$1.50 each	$1.40 each	$1.25 each
The Passion and The Death of Jesus Christ	$5.00 each	$1.60 each	$1.50 each	$1.20 each	$1.00 each	
The Incarnation, Birth and Infancy of Jesus Christ	$5.00 each	$1.60 each	$1.50 each	$1.20 each	$1.00 each	

Please enclose $4.00 for postage and handling for every 25 books.

Please write us for our booklist of 120 titles of the best Catholic Books.

Other fine books available at very low prices from:

Servants of Jesus and Mary
Nazareth Homestead
R.D. #1 Box 258
Constable, N.Y. 12926 U.S.A.

(703 pages) (506 pages) (502 pages) (469 pages)

The Eucharistic Miracle of Lanciano — See page 126